SPEAK
WITHOUT FEAR

Rock Star Presentation Skills

to Get People to Hear What You Say

SPEAK
WITHOUT FEAR

Rock Star Presentation Skills
to Get People to Hear What You Say

DEB SOFIELD

Firefly Printing Press ~ *Lighting your world one word at a time.*

Copyright © 2013 by Deb Sofield

Firefly Printing Press

Library of Congress Cataloging-in-Publication Data

ISBN: 978-0-9889483-0-3 eBook
ISBN: 978-0-6924203-3-1 Paperback

Although accurate web addresses were used at the time of publication, changes occur frequently online and these addresses are subject to change.

A NOTE TO READERS

Make no mistake: everyone is a public speaker to some degree. Most of us speak with the assumption that someone is listening. Otherwise, why should we speak at all? No one speaks with the goal of not being heard. It's evident, then, that we speak so that others will listen to what we have to say. If what we are saying is important enough, then our listener may remember what was said and, if it is worthy enough, may even repeat it.

I'm guessing you've picked up this particular book among many because you want to know how to speak without fear. That's part of what you'll learn, but the real trick to public speaking is to learn how to *speak and be heard*. Maybe you're a speaker by trade, maybe you're running for office, or maybe you need to gain confidence to be able to pipe up during monthly board meetings. Whatever your communication goals are, if you allow it, this book will help develop your delivery, your personal style, and the content of your message.

Public speaking is my life. Oftentimes businesses and organizations pay me a good deal of money to speak to their constituencies. I've been a public speaker and corporate trainer for twenty years, helping executives and elected officials to become capable and motivational speakers who deliver a message with lasting impact. I also serve as a visiting professor. I teach public speaking at John F. Kennedy School of Government at Harvard University, the Woman's Campaign School (where I am a past president of the board) at Yale University, the Southeastern Institute for Women in Politics, the University of South Carolina's School of Journalism and Mass Communications, Clemson University, and Furman University.

I know exactly what it takes—and means—to deliver a meaningful message. I know how empowering it is to speak confidently and boldly so that your audience hears what you say. And I understand what it means to fear you will not be heard. Whether you are speaking to one person or one thousand, this book will teach you how to overcome your particular obstacles to making yourself heard, and to speak without fear.

CONTENTS

The fear of public speaking is the number one phobia in the United States.

—The Book of Lists

INTRODUCTION

I like to say I became a public speaker because I wasn't good at anything else. That's not exactly true, but it's also not exactly untrue. When I look back at my career, and before that, my education, two things are abundantly clear: I'm good at talking, and I'm good at commanding the attention of others with my voice. These characteristics helped me to first become the owner of an advertising agency and later enter into politics. As a politician, I was motivated by the desire to effect change in people's lives, and committed to helping those who didn't have a voice. I have no trouble getting out and talking.

My first race was the state house. I knocked on four thousand doors, and spent a lot of time talking about what changes I was going to make. Not everything came easy to me, but I learned that nothing worth having comes easy. I lost my first race to an incumbent by one hundred and sixty-seven votes. Soon after, I ran for city council. I won every precinct in my district. I had one of the highest vote margins in a city election for my district.

I currently serve as the commissioner of public works for the water system for my city, which is an elected position, but what I learned from fourteen years of holding elected offices is that running for office is a lot like winning a beauty pageant. It's often not what you say. It's how you look; it's how you dress; it's how you carry yourself; and it's *how* you speak more than what you say.

In this book, I offer advice on what it takes to communicate effectively. Communication is an important ingredient of success in nearly every situation. When we communicate our thoughts and ideas to others, we forge a connection with people. This happens in job interviews, in business meetings, and in line at a coffee shop. Being able to communicate effectively, in order to achieve a desired outcome, is an important skill. Your rate of success in communication can make a difference in your salary, in an election, and in getting exactly what you want most of the time.

The art of effective communication comes naturally to some, while for others it is learned. Many people let fear get in the way of communicating effectively, especially when it comes to public speaking. However, public speaking doesn't always take place in front of large crowds, in auditoriums, or at a lectern. Phone calls, conference calls, and webinars all provide an opportunity to practice public speaking skills. People make presentations every day around the water cooler with colleagues, on planes, and at kids' soccer games. When it comes to coworkers, colleagues, teammates, friends, and family, especially children, it's paramount to communicate effectively. Being prepared for your presentation, and focusing on the delivery, will help you to communicate your message and your vision in any situation. In this book, you will find some of my "Fifteen Rules for the Road," a public speaking primer I developed over the course of my career, which are interspersed throughout the narrative, and which I have borrowed from my seminars. You will also find tips on how to speak formally and informally with passion, zeal, and conviction. You will learn how to be memorable (in good ways), how to make friends with your audience, and how to speak so that other people will listen.

The ultimate goal of this book is to teach you how to find your own, unique voice and learn to use it. This will enable you to articulate your thoughts well, which will make a difference in how others perceive you and how you perceive yourself. Your voice is an incredible instrument; I provide you with ways to make the most of it—to hone your vocal power. A strong command of your voice plays a big role in the way others perceive you and how you present yourself to the world. You will see how it is within your power to become an engaged and dynamic speaker. It is in your power to speak without fear, and it is in your power to be heard.

Section I:

WHAM
(WHAT HERE APPLIES TO ME)

Many people think that speeches only take place in an auditorium or at a conference in front of hundreds of people. The truth is that most of us give speeches every day, to large audiences, to small groups, across the table from a client at a restaurant, on the phone, at the computer, or in the elevator. If you can begin to understand public speaking in this way, you will gain more practice and confidence in the lessons you will learn from this book. If you begin to feel the grip of fear, remember that you do speak in public every day, and no one has died yet.

This section introduces concepts of communication, awareness (mostly of the self), observation (mostly of others), and what it means to have a message (believing what you say makes a difference). It's also essential to understand the concept of what I refer to as WHAM—"What here applies to me?"

In all exchanges, you should be able to answer the following: So what? Who cares? Should I be listening? Why is this important to me? You must be able to answer these questions within a few minutes, not just as a speaker, but also for your audience. You must be mindful that your audience is subconsciously saying, "Why should I listen? What will I learn? Why does this matter? What here applies to me?" As a speaker, you need to be able to answer those questions within the first few minutes of your presentation. You need to let the people you're speaking to know you're here for a reason, and more specifically, a reason that matters to them.

As speakers, the first chapter will help you understand the basics of communication, as the second chapter helps you move beyond mere verbal communication to better consider your overall presence and authenticity. When you're able to answer WHAM, you're able to offer your audience a road map of what to expect in their time with you. Once you're able to articulate WHAM, you'll be in the driver's seat of all that follows.

I

RETHINKING COMMUNICATION

Two monologues do not make a dialogue.
—JEFF DALY

People often ask me if just *anyone* can learn to speak. The answer, of course, is yes. Just like any other skill, everyone can learn to improve their public speaking abilities, and given the right amount of effort, preparation, and experience, everyone can learn to speak like a professional. It may not always be comfortable for just anyone to get up on stage and speak in front of a large audience, but learning to speak without fear is a process that begins with the speaker and his or her desire to reach out and share knowledge. A good speaker knows how to tell stories so that others can benefit from them. S o, yes, I believe that everyone can learn to speak—without fear—and I believe that the key to learning this is learning to perform like a rock star.

Public speaking opportunities can be some of the most rewarding experiences in an individual's lifetime. A chance to speak to a group is a chance to share knowledge with the world. During the time that an organization delegates to you, you will be the focus of a small population of people. You can spread your word and your vision by just getting up to the podium and sharing the thoughts that you have developed in your mind. When you see that your words have helped someone learn a new product or a new way of doing something; when you see that someone who is sitting before you will, because of your words, find strength for the journey; or if in your presentation you simply bring laughter to the world, you will feel a sense of awe and accomplishment. I have seen this happen often, among various speakers in front of diverse audiences.

Recalling to mind the fearful public speaker, the one who would rather do anything other than get up in front of a group of people to speak, think about the incredible sense of accomplishment you will have once it's over. Yes, it's important to win over your audience, but part of the practice of learning to speak without fear is simply getting up there and doing it. For those of you with butterflies in their stomachs, the task is more daunting, but you will reap the benefits more quickly.

For the speaker who does not necessarily tremble at the thought of speaking before an audience, but who fears a disconnect or a blunder during the speech, then the learning curve may be longer, or bumpier. It all depends on you and how much you are willing to put into the performance. It takes a lot of courage and confidence to sell yourself to an audience, and it takes a lot of enthusiasm to not just speak but to perform, especially on an otherwise tiresome day.

Regardless of your amount or type of fear, it's essential to start at the beginning: communication. Communication is simply the process of sharing information, feelings, and thoughts through speaking, writing, and body language. Most of us do this every day, so it seems simple, right? But have you ever received an e-mail, a text message, or a voice mail and thought, *What the heck does that mean?* Or maybe you've been on the receiving end of a message that was intended for someone else. As much as we communicate on a daily basis, *mis*communication is just as common. Whether it be not understanding that your wife wanted you to bring home a gallon of milk *and* a pound of butter or a pilot landing on the wrong runway because she mixed up the message from air control, funny (and frightening) stories of miscommunication abound when a message breaks down on the way from sender to receiver.

However, even garbled, misunderstood messages are classified as communication. They are simply not *effective* communication. Even if the message isn't a life-or-death situation, we should all make sure we are communicating effectively. It isn't that difficult, but it does require some thought, planning, and practice.

Straight out of college, I was given a survey list. On the list were ten skills expected of a potential employee. The list contained all sorts of the so-called "hard" technical skills like finance, operations, project management, software development, human resource management, and so forth. The list also contained a few "soft" skills like communications, interpersonal relationship, and leadership skills. I was asked to pretend I was the CEO of an organization and to rank the skills in order of their importance in an employee. I remember thinking project management was a great skill to have, followed by human resource management knowledge, and so on. I ranked all the hard skills over the soft skills.

It turns out the top CEOs of the Fortune 500 had taken the survey, and they had all ranked the soft skills at the top. Communication skills were the highest-ranked aggregate of the skills for a new hire, followed by interpersonal skills, and then leadership. It seems communications and positive peer-to-peer interactions are more valuable, or at least more difficult to teach, than technical, hard skills. This truly underlines the point that it doesn't matter what you know if you can't effectively communicate or get along well with others. In this book, I will share many of my own secrets to effective communication that have come from years of experience in a variety of settings so that you *can* learn to communicate effectively.

Remember the game Telephone? Participants sit in a circle, and the first person on the phone is in charge of creating a message. Then each person whispers the message around the circle before the last person says the message aloud. When I played in kindergarten, the message was usually garbled and nonsensical, and it made us all giggle. As I tell this story now, I realize what a wonderful lesson it was in learning to communicate: to enunciate words, to speak clearly, and to speak with intention; otherwise the kid sitting next to you might call you out as the one who had messed up. As a kid, I thought we were just having fun, but we were actually participating in a lesson on effective communication.

At that very young age, children learn that if they want others to hear what they are saying, they must communicate their message effectively. These communication skills will shape the perception that our teachers, classmates, and other parents form about us—and they can define an entire academic career. If you were a shy student, have no fear. It is not too late to learn, and it's more important than ever. As an adult, your ability to communicate with others defines many aspects of your livelihood, including relationships with family, friends, and coworkers.

In my years of public speaking, I have met many individuals who have shared with me their personal success stories in learning to communicate effectively. I remember these stories because they are meaningful to me and I can relate to them. When this happens, not only do I remember the person and the story, but I often like to repeat it.

A recent college graduate told me a story about how he had learned to overcome his fear of speaking a foreign language. He had studied the language for years in books and in classes, but he was struggling to overcome his fear of speaking it. While studying abroad one semester, he watched a fellow American, who didn't seem to know more about the language than he did, *act* as if she were a native speaker. He had an eye-opening moment when he realized that there is much more to speaking than knowing grammar or vocabulary. There is confidence, intonation, inflection, and a little bit of pizzazz thrown together to make it complete.

Yes, communication is the process of sharing information. However, we share much more than just basic facts; we also share feelings and thoughts, which often come across through the conscious or subconscious use of body language. How many times have you shaken your head in frustration (or worse) because the receiver didn't understand your message? This frustration often manifests itself in subtle ways.

Have you ever assigned a task to someone only to have him or her do something else? Did you think that person might be daft, dumb, or lazy? Well, that might have been the case, but more often than not, it was a result of miscommunication, and the miscommunication was a result of the way you sent the message. If this has happened to you, ask yourself, *Did my message effectively communicate my thoughts and desires?* It's a good rule of thumb to question yourself before you question your listener. It's likely that the listener responded and acted according to what he or she understood.

Consider the story of the frustrated dog trainer. A woman was going on vacation to Europe and left her four-legged companion with a popular kennel. This kennel was known for its friendly staff, large play area, and top-notch trainers, who offered complimentary obedience training with every stay. When the woman returned to pick up her pooch, the front desk clerk relayed a message from the trainer. The trainer had been frustrated with the dog's unwillingness to obey even the most simple of commands. The woman looked down at her dog and said, "¡*Sientate!*" and the dog promptly sat down and waited for the next command. The dog had been trained in Spain and knew over fifty commands—in Spanish, the woman told the clerk. The problem was not the dog's unwillingness to listen; the trainer was just not speaking his language. We must know our audience and be able to communicate to them in a language they understand. Whether it means using age-appropriate language while speaking to children, or using the correct technical terminology while speaking in front of a group of physicists at a conference, understanding your audience and using a vocabulary they understand will help you avoid miscommunications. Because let's face it; when you argue with a dog, you're the only one who looks silly.

We've all had the experience of being in an argument with someone, whether it be a parent, child, partner, or friend. If we think about it, arguments rarely come about because we have totally different outlooks or desires. Because these are people we care about and who care about us. We want what is best for each other and we want each other to be happy. Yet miscommunication causes us to think we are on opposite ends of the spectrum. We think our spouse would rather work than spend time with us, when instead he or she is concerned with finances or focused on getting a promotion. If we take time to communicate with each other, our spouse learns that we need some quality time, while we learn that he or she needs support and encouragement to spend a little extra time at work until the finances are straightened out or the promotion is earned.

In this Information Age, we have unlimited opportunities to communicate with people all over the world. Sadly, most people use these opportunities to rant, rather than to listen and try to understand. I'm sure you've read an angry comment on a controversial article or blog, which then sparked more angry comments. The angry and insulting tone of many of these comments makes it almost impossible to respond with respect. If the comments had been written in a more respectful way, we might respond by taking the time to understand the reasons behind the particular political or religious belief. Our response would probably be, "Oh. I never thought about it that way." We still might not agree, but at least we'd realize that the other conclusion makes sense based on where the writer is coming from.

Or how about being blamed for something you didn't do, or that was the result of someone else's misinformation? It is frustating not to be heard or understood. It is even more frustating if someone refuses to listen to our explanation.

Miscommunications can take many forms. If I speak to you in sign language and you don't understand me, I am still communicating with you, but a key ingredient is missing. If I tell you in sign language that I saw a large snake crawl into your car, you might look at me strangely, then proceed to get in your car anyway. I could just shrug my shoulders and walk off, or I could interpret your strange look to mean that you didn't understand me. In that case, I could pull out a pen and a piece of paper, run over to you, and quickly write,

"I saw a large snake crawl into your car. You may not want to get inside just yet." Then I could reevaluate the level of comprehension and ascertain whether you understood my message.

Components of Effective Communication

There are six major components of the communication process: the context, the sender, the message, the channel, the receiver, and the feedback. (See figure below.) The process is a loop, and feedback from the receiver (or listener) keeps it going.

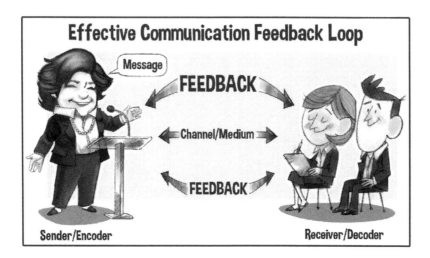

The context is the setting, or circumstances, in which an idea develops. In the example of the snake in the car, the context might have been that I witnessed a snake slithering into your car, which would probably manifest itself as urgency. The context within which a message is formulated begins the communication process. Now, it is my responsibility as the sender to make sure you, the receiver, *receive* the correct message. I do this through various channels or mediums, such as words, symbols, gestures, or other body language to convey the message *and* to produce feedback from you. Trying to prevent you from entering your car, I might shout, jump up and down, wave my arms in the air, and even run toward the car to make sure you can hear me.

This example requires that I react quickly and instinctively to communicate a warning. When it comes to communicating an important but non-urgent message, however, a good speaker will take time to consider the context, verbal and nonverbal clues, and as many other extraneous context items as possible before sending the message.

I am most aware of this when sending and receiving emails or listening to someone I don't know give a presentation. We all know how easy, and frustrating, it is to be misunderstood. Because I am so aware that emails can be often misinterpreted, I take time to make sure my message is crafted for maximum understandability. If I receive a questionable email, I take the time to contact the sender directly and make sure I haven't misinterpreted something. Similarly, when I'm listening to someone I don't know give a presentation, I concentrate on *how the message is being offered* as much as I do *the message itself* in order to ensure I'm receiving the message the speaker intends for me to receive. In public speaking, good, effective communicators use many of the same skills. They take the time to craft their speech and words to fit the *context* and to reduce misinterpretation.

The *message* is the idea that the sender crafts and transmits to the receiver. The *channel* is the mechanism used to communicate this message. It could be a voice or a flashing sign in Times Square. Whichever channel the sender chooses, the goal is for the receiver to accurately understand the sender's message, just as in the children's game Telephone that I described earlier. In the game, the receiver is the one who keeps the game moving along. The receiver's anticipation of the message will prepare him or her to listen carefully.

A successful, effective sender will consider the receiver's knowledge of the subject when crafting and delivering the message. For example, in the game, if there is a new, big word in the message, an effective communicator may enunciate and say that word more slowly than the other words contained in the message. A good listener will respond to the speaker's change in intonation and inflection, and may offer feedback accordingly. You can imagine, in a kindergarten class, the five-year-old shouting back with a giggle at the sender, "What?" upon hearing the unfamiliar word.

Feedback is what creates the loop in the figure. Feedback may take the form of verbal or nonverbal responses, as in a question, a nod, nervous giggle, or a frustrated groan. The sender may then respond by repeating his or her message. Effective communication is a two-way street. It requires intention on behalf of the sender in establishing the context, crafting the message, and choosing the channel. It also requires feedback on the part of the receiver.

Barriers to Effective Communication

Imagine a bull is charging toward you, and you are trying to tell your coworker the guidelines for a new project that you are working on together. The context of the approaching bull should serve as a warning that it is not an ideal time to practice effective communication.

- A breakdown in communication may result if the sender fails to recognize the full context of the receiver's state of mind. Pay attention to body language and the setting before delivering an important message. If a coworker or customer comes to you in an angry state, you may just want to listen to allow the person the opportunity to vent. In that state of mind, she isn't going to be a very effective decoder of your message.

- Spouting out too much information too quickly may be another barrier to effective communication. Instead of telling someone face-to-face the twenty-seven steps he needs to do, you can choose another channel and provide it in writing. This also allows the receiver to decode a lengthy message in his own time.

- If the sender has a poor understanding of the subject matter, then the receiver is going to have a difficult time decoding the message.

Some barriers to effective communication are like static on a radio or poor cell phone reception, and can block the clear delivery of the message. I was once driving to a dinner party and needed to call the host several times to get detailed directions. The house was out in the country and the cell phone reception was spotty at best and he had to repeat himself because he kept breaking up. Due to the poor connection, I could only hear bits and pieces of the message.

- Physical distractions, like actual background noise, act as barriers. Crowds, multitasking, environmental issues like poor weather, and technical difficulties can all impede a sender's message.

- Another barrier can be poor grammar or language skills. It may be difficult to interpret a message if the message is garbled or worded incorrectly. Years ago when a friend was running for Congress another friend made it clear she'd never vote for someone so stupid. Her evidence—and I'm guessing since the friend lost his bid others may have agreed—was that he pronounced "government," as "gubment," and there was no way she was going to "send another Southern politician to Washington so he could sound dumb on *Meet the Press*."

- Sometimes a message may conflict with other messages, and sometimes a sender may actually contradict herself in the course of a message. In the business environment, message conflict can occur when technical terms, jargon, or acronyms are used instead of clearly stating the information.

- Anyone who has ever tried to talk to, or remembers being, a teenager will understand how attitude can affect communication. The attitude can block the sender or the receiver from the message and in some cases completely change the meaning according to one's own agenda.

- Child-speak is what I call it when adults speak down to children, otherwise known as baby talk. Though you might want to consider simplifying it for your audience, you shouldn't "dumb down" your message. Although you must take your audience into consideration, if you dumb down your audience, you eventually dumb down yourself.

I remember coming home one day and finding a note on the refrigerator that said, "Ran to the store. Don't forget to be ready for tonight. Back soon." My mind quickly processed two things. One, I had no idea what was happening that night. And two, I knew I couldn't contact the sender to inquire—it was before cell phones. Instead, I panicked and racked my brain trying to figure out what was happening that night.

In situations like this, feedback from the receiver is impossible, but the sender can take some precautions to make sure his or her message is clear and unambiguous. The note could have said, "Ran to the store. Remember we have dinner at the neighbors' at seven o'clock." The sender of the original message did not take into account that I had just arrived home after a long business trip and that I would unlikely be able to decode the message properly. As a result, my anxiety level shot up.

It doesn't help the process to become anxious or angry if the receiver is having trouble understanding the message. This would never fly at a public speaking event. Remember, the onus is on the sender to make sure all of the variables are present for effective communication. Frustration on behalf of the sender or receiver will not help the communication process at all. As a sender, you are not able to control the receiver's attitude, but you are able to control your own.

Be Bold, Your Body Is Talking

How we communicate with our bodies accounts for more information transfer between humans than you might think. Harvard Business School professor Amy Cuddy holds a PhD in psychology and has done research to the effect that just two minutes in an open pose (sitting up straight, standing with hands on hips) actually boosts your testosterone and lowers your cortisol levels, while two minutes in a closed position (slouching, arms crossed) does the opposite, affecting not just the impression of power and confidence but the actual physical presence of them. Between 60 and 80 percent of human communication is nonverbal; Dr. James Borg, author of *Body Language and Persuasion: The Art of Influencing People*, even suggests that as high as 93 percent of communication in human interaction is derived from nonverbal cues and only 7 percent from words themselves.

When people talk about their ability to read people and situations, they are referring to paralinguistics, which is the study of vocal and nonvocal signals that go beyond speech. Some people assimilate non-verbal and other paralinguistic cues readily and are able to develop a mental image or understanding of an individual, group, or situation based on this nonverbal language.

Sometimes people mirror or mimic another person's body language to indicate that they understand the message, or that they agree with the speaker. However, not all body language is meant for communication, and just as with words, a receiver may misconstrue or misinterpret body language.

I teach my students to use body language in a professional situation to show a powerful presence, interest, agreement, and understanding. If you are seated, lean ever so slightly forward to show engagement. People who are actively engaged naturally lean forward to absorb the conversation or situation. When interacting with others, always maintain eye contact to show engagement. A verbal nod or controlled nod of the head will also show the sender that you are engaged. Always try to avoid slouching, fidgeting, and harsh, blank, or bored facial expressions. These may happen unconsciously, but they can have a big impact on whether or not someone is receptive to your message.

Even though nonverbal cues are a tremendous indicator of context and are part of the message, they are *not* the message. In the professional world, the message is often about sharing detailed information or directions with one, or many. If you use confusing or conflicting nonverbal cues, you may ruin the message because your words are saying one thing and your body another.

I sometimes look at my dog, who despite my best wishes does not speak English very well, and reflect on just how important these non-verbal cues are. Sure, he knows and understands his name and a few other words, like "ball," but for the most part, he lives in a world of nonverbal communication. He responds to the tone of my voice and the gestures that I use. I can pat him on the head and say in my sweetest, most gentle voice, "You are a very bad dog. I am very disappointed in you." While I am saying this, his tail is wagging ferociously. I then say to him in my harshest, angry voice, "You are the sweetest dog in the world. You are such a good dog!" and his little tail will curl up while his gaze is averted to the floor.

If you don't pay attention to nonverbal cues, an important message may get lost in the noise. It is possible to learn and practice certain skills to make sure that nonverbal noise doesn't obscure an intended message. How can one accomplish this? Learn to read nonverbal cues from others, and learn to deliver intentional nonverbal cues.

Learning to read nonverbal clues can be fun, too. I love to people-watch. It helps that I travel a lot and often dine alone. I have an active imagination and will watch people interact to see if I can read their body language.

Learn to Read Nonverbal Cues:

- Practice people-watching and see if you can tell what people are talking about without listening to their conversation.
- Don't put too much emphasis on one particular gesture. We've all crossed our arms unconsciously without intending to send a signal of hostility. Look at nonverbal cues as a group of gestures instead of focusing on one.
- Be aware of differences: cultural, age, geo-location, and gender differences can all play a part in the different use of gestures and other nonverbal cues.

Pay attention to the delivery of nonverbal cues. Practice and watch reactions when you use certain gestures, stances, or postures. While traveling, I get to work on my nonverbal soft skills with strangers and people who speak different languages than I do. I haven't tried my dog trick with a human being yet, but I do sometimes deliver the same question to multiple people in different ways. Sometimes I will cross my arms or act bored when asking a question of a hotel receptionist. Other times, I will ask the same question by leaning forward and acting like I am extremely interested in their feedback. With practice you can learn to deliver the right nonverbal cues.

Learn to Deliver Nonverbal Cues:

- Practice delivering your nonverbal cues in the appropriate context. Watch how people interact with children, and practice speaking with children. Children are fantastic observers and use a higher percentage of nonverbal cues to determine meaning. They will show you, either with body language or words, if you are giving them mixed signals.
- Learn to deliver positive nonverbal cues even in situations where you aren't necessarily feeling so self-assured. During a difficult interview or presentation, I have had to work hard to conceal fear in order to project calm and confidence.

Learn to Listen to Be Heard

I was recently involved in a conference call with perhaps twenty people on the call and five or six of us in the room. I was there as a consultant and was not responsible for running the meeting. The person running the meeting did an amazing job. There were different levels of political power in the room, so there were many facets of communication to consider.

What impressed me the most was this person's ability to effectively run the meeting. He listened carefully and provided detailed feedback. If he was unsure that everyone on the call or in the room understood something, he would interrupt and say, "I'm sorry to cut in here, but what I heard was 'we need to finish a, b, and c first, then we can concentrate on finishing d, e, and f.' Is that correct?" This technique allowed everyone who hadn't understood the chance to either hear the information anew.

This reflexive technique of repeating or mirroring information back to the sender is a great way to ensure group understanding. It is also a technique used to mitigate the psychological phenomena known as groupthink. Groupthink occurs when a desire for group harmony overrides realistic and appropriate views of the situation.

A tragic and notable example of groupthink occurred days and weeks before the space shuttle *Challenger* disaster. In a room full of gifted and extremely intelligent engineers, scientists, and astronauts, no one voiced their concern about the effect the freezing temperatures might have on the fuel tank seals. When interviewed individually, almost every single member of the group voiced a concern about the temperature and the seals, yet no one ever voiced their concern to the group as a whole. The consensus was "If the other members didn't feel it was a big enough deal to mention, then why should I?" The results were catastrophic. The proper question was never asked, and no one bothered to listen or speak up until it was too late.

Listening is not only important to effective communication; it can also save lives. When someone calls 911 in an emergency, the operator who answers must be fully focused on the call. He must listen to what the caller is saying, and must often ask the caller to repeat where she lives or what is happening. Taking a 911 call while distracted could mean the difference between getting life-saving help to someone in time or not.

While most of our day-to-day opportunities to listen do not involve life-or-death situations, listening is more important than we realize. I used to think that I engaged in active listening every time I paid attention to what someone was saying, but that just wasn't the case. In most cases, I was only half-listening. Once I realized that I was missing out on what the speaker was saying, I began to practice deeper concentration and learned to decrease the noise barrier and increase my listening capacity.

- Learn to project your interest to the sender by showing him you are engaged in what he has to say. A controlled nod, smiling, and making solid eye contact lets the sender know you are ready to receive his message.

- Make sure you don't roll your eyes, allow your mind to wander, or otherwise project your non-interest to the sender.

- The hardest thing you will ever do is to let the sender finish before you give your feedback. Unless it is a life-or-death situation and every second is critical, you need to avoid interrupting the sender until her message has finished. Allowing someone to finish their thoughts is a form of validation. It lets the sender know that you respect and value their message.

- The term "jumping to conclusions" was probably coined in response to someone interrupting a sender before his message was done. You are also nonverbally screaming to the sender that he is insignificant.

- Don't be dismissive. Wait, listen—really take a moment to ponder—then respond.
- Don't talk over someone or upstage her with what you have to say. Sometimes allowing someone to have their moment in the sun is a gift you can give that costs you nothing but is a reflection of your kindness.
- You cannot be a good listener if you are thinking about what you are going to say while the other person is still talking.

In order to be a world-class speaker, presenter, businessperson, or even a successful human being, you must learn to evaluate a given context, craft a strong message, chose a strong channel, and assess your receiver's ability to receive your message. Gesturing, pointing, and yelling may get your point across eventually (remember the snake in the car?) but you want to learn to develop healthy, positive, two-way-street relationships with the people around you: your audience, your family, or your coworkers.

Pay attention to context. It is an important component in the communication loop. Remember to seek feedback. It keeps the loop going. If you are the sender, expect and ask for feedback for message comprehension. If you are the receiver, reflexively provide feedback by stating what you heard the message to be.

Practice your soft, nonverbal skills. Even if yours are a little rough, they can be honed and improved. I hope you know now how important they are. Remember that the CEOs of top companies value your communication ability more than they value what you know.

2

BEING BIG

Talkers have always ruled. They will continue to rule.
The smart thing is to join them.
—BRUCE BARTON

There's something Glenn Beck, Chelsea Handler, Prince, Nancy Grace, Donald Trump, and Chris Christie have in common. Whether you love 'em or hate 'em, they're authentic and they know how to take up personal space and be big. You know the type. At least you know it when you see it. Sometimes this sense of presence is difficult to put into words, but there's no doubt you recognize it when it's in the room. When you're near it, you take notice and pay attention; we all do. Some of us call it star quality.

The first step in defining or upping your personal sha-bang factor is to quiet that naysaying voice in your head that pipes up with some nonsense about your lack of "star quality." Everyone has sha-bang. Everyone has something-something—that *je ne sais quoi* that makes them irrevocably unique, distinct, and unerringly one of a kind. If you're human, you have star quality. Don't get me wrong—it may be pinned under layers and layers of self-loathing or regret or fear or indifference or apathy, but absolutely everyone has some amount of it. So while you might want to say you're either born with it or not—you either have it or you don't—I'm here to tell you that star quality can be something you work at. It can be something you hone. Winston Churchill and Lady Gaga were not built in a day.

It doesn't even have to come naturally, not at first. It's attainable. It can be something gradual—something you work at like chess or rolling sushi. No big leaps of faith necessary. If you want to become more authentic, take the first step. Without a doubt, it's yours to take. It's the same thing with star quality. Once you begin to sing your own song (I mean this metaphorically—that is, unless you're a singer, then by all means, sing what you're meant to sing) and embrace what makes you original, you'll be well on your way. Oscar Wilde said, "Most people are other people. Their thoughts are someone else's opinions, their lives a mimicry, their passions a quotation." Once you become your thoughts and live your own opinions and passions, you become authentic, and once you're authentic, you'll have a much better chance at being big—and powerful.

Show the World What You've Got: Three Types of Star Quality

When it comes to being big, there are three kinds of people: those who take names, those who need a nudge, and those who need to leave it at the river. What tribe you fall into has a lot to do with how you were raised, your education, your sense of worth, and how comfortable you are in your own skin. Have you ever noticed how natural most young children are? Consider a four- or five-year-old. The world hasn't yet made them bend. They don't use hair gel;

they don't wear belts; they have utter and unyielding acceptance of their place in the world. They don't question whether or not someone wants to hear their opinion; they give it freely and with wild abandon.

Some of us can tap into that sense of self-empowerment without any trouble, and I think these people have a better sense of wonderment, innocence, and power. *Of course folks will listen to me. Of course my boss wants to hear what I have to say. Of course what I have to say is important and meaningful. Of course I can make a difference. Of course, of course, of course!* There are others who are more timid; still others who find it actually painful to take the leap into showing the world what they have to offer. Regardless of where you're at on the star-quality spectrum, you can improve, and your first step is to consider where it is you stand.

Those Who Take Names

If you're someone who knows you have something to say and feels absolutely no fear when it comes to screaming whatever's on your mind from the rooftops—that's great. If you have very little doubt others will listen to you—even better. Natural confidence gives you a leg up on things. It means you're more willing to share your accomplishments with others (even better is if you're the sort of person who can give compliments and build others up as well). It means you're usually willing to offer your opinion (unfortunately, this doesn't mean you're always right, but the good news is if you *are* right folks will know about it). It doesn't mean you're perfect, just that *you feel worthy.* The squeaky wheel often gets the grease, so if you're one of Those Who Take Names, then you also want to make sure you're not bulldozing over your brethren—just because you have a voice doesn't mean you don't have to listen. Still, feeling worthy is half the battle and often means you're well ahead of the game and ready to kick butt and make a difference.

Those Who Need a Nudge

All of us bring something to the table. Maybe you're the sort of worker bee who really is cut out for middle management—and there's nothing wrong with that. Maybe you like to be a part of a team and you don't have to be the end-all be-all of the group. Maybe you like having a supporting role and you're not necessarily the sort of person to speak up, at least not at first or unless you really feel like something needs to be said and no one else is saying it. Maybe your confidence is a little off—or maybe you're simply the quiet type. If you are one of Those Who Need a Nudge, speaking without fear isn't an option; it's a matter of having control over the butterflies fluttering around your nerved-out stomach lining. The thing is, you've been successful before, and you can be successful with this. Just because you're one of Those Who Need a Nudge doesn't mean you can't speak with power, clarity, and believable conviction. Those Who Need a Nudge are usually good at crafting articulate and well-considered presentations; it's simply a matter of tweaking the delivery and learning a few tricks of the public-speaking trade.

Those Who Need to Leave It at the River

I grew up in the South—a gift of which I'm ever grateful. We ate family dinners, went to church every Sunday, and never wore white after Labor Day. In that mix of Southern culture, my brothers and I were blessed with a wonderful housekeeper named Annie Belle. Annie Belle had a way of saying things. A bit of wisdom she offered when I was a child and, later, teen distress was to: leave it by the river and don't pick it up again. The missive stuck. When I'm burdened by a stress I can't do anything about, I do exactly as Annie Belle taught me. If you're carrying something you're not meant to carry, I want you to do the same: leave it at the river.

Some people never had a cheering section to tell them they were special. Maybe something happened in their childhoods. Maybe they've been rocked by a divorce or abuse or a death of someone they loved—there are countless reasons to feel inadequate. Whatever it is that takes a person to a place of perpetual self-doubt, perpetual second-guessing, and a life of perpetual fear, it's time to leave it at the river. If it's up to you to scream "Fire!" in order to save lives but you find yourself too meek to make a peep, it's time to leave it at the river.

Being fearful comes from overthinking—so Those Who Need to Leave It at the River need to begin reconsidering their mental game. Look at it this way: when you're called to share a message— and this can be any sort of message—don't dare miss the opportunity because you don't feel good about yourself. The sneaking voice in the back of your head is wrong. Leave whatever baggage you have at the door. Naomi Wolf was right: we are entitled to wear cowboy boots to our own revolution.

Meet Mr. and Ms. Big

Your first tip in being big is to accept the fact that there's often a lot of judgment from your peers. Taking up space may mean making a few folks uncomfortable (and that's OK). It's about having a firm handshake. Whether you're a man or a woman, it's about respect and offering a generously warm welcome. Ladies and gentleman, if your mother taught you it was only required that men stand when someone joins your table, let me tell you: times have changed. It's essential we show respect for one another—regardless of how formal or informal the gathering—by rising to the occasion. That's right. If someone joins the group—be it business luncheon or board meeting—take a stand.

For you to find your space, you need to be a player on the court and not a spectator in the stands. The only way you will be seen as successful and powerful is to fill the space. You will lose your position of power if you are seen as a spectator. You and I both know that someone else will fill the space and take the credit if you don't. If you want to make a difference, get in the game. We don't want wallflowers. We don't want pansies. We want Superwoman to stand up and look us in the eyes and Superman to stand up straight and make things happen. It's time to meet Mr. and Mrs. Big.

More than star quality, becoming Mr. or Mrs. Big means optimizing what you've got—and ensuring you've got plenty of elbowroom. I've never met a trailblazer who wasn't authentic. Be who "they" want and need you to be, but be yourself. It's a mindset.

How you see yourself ultimately defines how others perceive you, but more than merely mindset, it's also about your actions. Carry yourself with strength and power. Don't shrink back—you'll be overlooked. Understand that from the minute you walk into a business setting, or really any setting for that matter, everything—from how you pull out your chair and sit down to how you say "so long and farewell"—is being graded. (We'll look more closely into exactly how we're graded in Section II: First, Second, and Third Impressions.)

I can't say it enough: *powerful people take up physical space*™. In this book, in this life, and in your presentations—no slouching is allowed. Move around, smile, make eye contact, feel the beat of humanity's inner drum. Pay attention. Ultimately, people will gain confidence in you when you have confidence in yourself. Being shy, insecure, and passive gets you nowhere. So take a seat at the table—front and center—and clear space for yourself. Do not cede your position of power. Take up space and remember that powerful people take up physical space and *own it*.

Men are often better at this than women. Women are taught that the smaller we are the prettier we appear. This is killing women in the business world. Most women were taught to be little princesses—not little bruisers. How do women stand for a photo? Sideways (we look thinner that way) and demure, but I guarantee no one looks at a sideways photo and is able to point to who's in charge. Consider men. When they take a photo, they're usually positioned straight on. Have you ever seen a photo of Oprah Winfrey, Hillary Clinton, Condi Rice, or Meg Whitman? No one crowds them out—not ever. So here it is: own your space; don't share your space—it's yours. I'm inviting you to the party.

Your "Likability Factor"

Gallup Polls conducts over a thousand interviews each day, 350 days out of the year, on landline and cell phones across the US. They have successfully predicted presidential elections based on measuring the public's perception of presidential candidates since 1936 (notable exceptions include the 1948 Thomas Dewey–Harry S. Truman election, where nearly all pollsters predicted a Dewey victory, and the 1976 election where they inaccurately projected a slim victory by Gerald Ford, when he lost to Jimmy Carter by a small margin). It's telling proof that we vote for the candidate we like best. Studies also show we do business with the people we like best—even when they might not be the best contenders. So it makes a good bit of sense that a speaker can win over an audience if he or she appears likable. (At the very least, you'll get a vote or work, even if it's not what you're shooting for.)

Likability can make up for a lot of mistakes. Think about reality TV shows like *Survivor* and *The Bachelor*. They're based on likability, not accomplishment—who the audience likes and who they vote off the show, which potential fiancée the bachelor finds most appealing on any number of levels. Or how about the numerous romantic comedies in which the underdog gets the girl, despite mistakes and misunderstandings, simply because he is more likable than the guy with the six-figure salary or the smooth charm or the famous career. Look at Bill Clinton, Tiger Woods, Michael Phelps, Martha Stewart, and Ellen DeGeneres. Likability wins every time.

Likability begins with liking who you are and what you stand for. When you truly believe that you're worth liking and worth listening to, that's when people begin to take notice. If you love yourself, your audience will love you.

Specific Tools to Set Your Fears Aside

Set your fear aside. I hear you saying, "Come on, Deb, that's easier said then done." And you're right. Fear creates a block in people that's often really difficult to move past. Notice that I said *difficult*, not *impossible*. As with all obstacles, we must have a reason to take them on, conquer, and move past. If you really want to be a speaker, there's a reason that's bigger than your fear, which means that you *can* overcome your fear. And know this: just because you're afraid doesn't mean there's something wrong with you. *Every* speaker starts out with some apprehension. The trick is to channel that nervous energy into your presentation, and when you do that, fear manifests as power.

I tell my clients to "pull their other self out." Find the strong, courageous, loving, bright "other self" and let that person do the talking. If I ever feel fear, I pull myself out of myself. I let this "other self" stand next to me (I know it's getting pretty esoteric here, but stay with me) and tell this other self next to me that she has a message to give and that the message is needed to change lives and give people a chance to succeed. When I do this, I set aside all of the fears that existed in the old me. The speech is not really about me. Let me repeat that: *It is not about me.* I have a message for my audience, one that will help them realize their strengths and become powerful speakers. The message is what empowers people, and even if they don't like me, Deb Sofield, they'll love my message because they need my message.

To speak without fear is to realize that your speech is not about you; it's about the listener. Your job is to find ways to reach listeners. You're only here to help, and although it may be one of your ulterior hopes, your audience doesn't have to like you for you to empower them. This is the key to learning to speak without fear. No matter how personal it feels, remember, it's not about you; it's first and foremost about your message. Your message is what truly matters. Your message is what your audience will get passionate about. After all, it's what *you* are passionate about!

When it comes to quelling the jitters, sometimes you just have to "do it afraid" to learn that you don't have to be afraid. That's what my brothers said when they taught me to water ski. Their motivation for doing this was that when I fell, they could honestly tell my parents they lost me in the lake. They threw me out of the boat, tossed me the skis, and told me, from the comfort of the boat, how to put them on, how to hold the rope, and what to expect. I remember that I was afraid because I don't like lakes with their muddy, squishy, cold bottoms. I was afraid of the water because I couldn't see through it. I was afraid because I thought the fish in the lake would get me. I was especially worried about the piranhas one of my brothers told me some kid had dumped in the lake the day before. One of my brothers offered me his hand—not to pull me from the water, but to help me focus on my fears. He told me that they were unfounded: specifically that my life vest made it impossible to drown and that piranhas don't live in freshwater. Then they all agreed that I could get back in the boat if I just got up one time on the skis. If I got up once, my trial would be over.

I bet you can imagine how this scenario ended. Once I finally got up on those skis, I had so much fun that I wouldn't get back in the boat. My fear had turned into passion. I had faced what I was afraid of and discovered that it couldn't defeat me, that it wasn't impossible, and that I was actually *good* at it! This is why we have to "do things afraid"—so we can discover not only what we're good at, but that we can have fun doing it.

Faith Language

I'm often brought into political campaigns because I understand "faith language": it's not what you believe, but the how and why. There's vagueness to such concepts, but I've found nearly everyone, especially when it comes to business and politics, wants to make a human connection.

Faith language connects like-minded folks who you'd never know by name or face (and wouldn't necessarily have an opportunity to find in a crowd), but *through your language* (your choices in words and phrases), you'll nearly instantly befriend. This is a good thing to keep in mind as you make your way through the world. Enlisting—listening to and being informed by—faith language allows me to figure out at any given conference the drinkers from the teetotalers, the early-risers from those who are prone to dance until dawn, the gym rats and runners, the foodies. We all connect by using phrases that say what we need to say without explaining. It's a part of recognizing one's tribe.

I offer this example. Because I grew up in the church and my faith is important to me, I often pepper my messages with Bible verses, such as "train a child in the way he should go," "amazing grace, how sweet the sound," "surely goodness and mercy will follow me all the days of my life." These phrases, and thousands more, act as a connector to my "faith" community (in this case, literally and figuratively). To a lot of folks in my audience, these phrases merely sound like nice words of wisdom, and they are, but for a select few, those phrases serve as our connector.

As speakers, we want our audience to listen to us and respond to us. Sometimes we may speak in order to educate a group, to be a cheerleader, or to impart information for information's sake. It is helpful to know what the expected outcome is in order to craft a successful presentation. As you put your thoughts down on paper, include details about the expectations of your presentation and the group to whom you will be speaking. This will help you to think about what you hope their response will be. If you can set up the expectation within your speech, many times success will follow. I recently heard Xavier Cartiaux, president of international operations at ScanSource, Inc., on a business panel I was moderating say it best: "Catching the heart is more powerful than commanding the hands." He's right; once you capture the heart of your audience, their response will be tangible.

We've all believed in something—or at least I hope we are striving to be there someday—bigger than our own small biospheres, things beyond our front step. Those moments in our life that are bigger than any single one of us are, well, grand.

Look at the Higgs boson particle recently discovered. What's amazing to me is not just that it explains how matter attains its mass; it's that the particle has been the subject of a forty-five-year hunt. It's taken loads and loads of researchers and scientists; men and women have spent their careers in pursuit of it. It's been something to believe in for so many people, and that belief has inspired their hard work and dedication in pursuit of it. Now their hard work and their belief are being rewarded; they have discovered something truly significant.

Maybe there's not international significance to what your message holds. Maybe you're trying to get more parents to volunteer their time at school events, or maybe you're trying to increase sales at your car lot. In any event, what you say isn't really always about you—of course, it's about the message, and what your message needs is a rock star with stage presence.

When I speak about having a powerful presence and understanding group dynamics of perceptions of power, I like to tell this story. I can tell from experience that where you sit at the table will solidify your position of power in the eyes of others. If you have the confidence to sit where everyone will see you, then you will naturally show a powerful presence.

So where do you get the strength to invite yourself to the table? Well, I have two theories. First, when you were a little kid, you swallowed a penny. You may not remember, but you did. That money got inside of you and it grew. That's what I call self-worth. Some of you swallowed a lot of pennies and you grew up fine, but others didn't swallow enough to have the self-confidence to believe in their rightful position of power. My other theory is this: When we were younger, many of us had someone—it might have been a parent, or a teacher, or a coach—who made it a priority to build our confidence every day. They told us often with many words of encouragement that we could be and do anything we put our minds to; they built us up and deposited coins of praise, admiration, and kindness. If you heard that you were significant, amazing, and special when you were growing up, then it's likely that you are doing your life's work. It makes a big difference that someone believed in you. Not coincidently, it also makes it easier to carry the torch of a healthy self-esteem and spark that self-worth in others.

Unfortunately not everyone grew up with that type of encouragement. Positive reinforcement wasn't always the norm, and some of us didn't hear those reassuring words of affirmation when the going got tough. For those who did not have that gift, I will tell you a secret. It is one to which many subscribe. Sometimes you have to fake till you make it.

This is a fact. Don't let a lack of self-confidence damage your career. That's your own perception of your self-worth. Sit at the table and take up space. The great thing about speaking from personal experience is that you won't need a cue card—you tell it from memory.

Section II:

FIRST, SECOND, AND
THIRD IMPRESSIONS

*Merrie Spaeth, author of Marketplace Communications, states that:
"Television is crucially important to today's executives because it has
shaped the expectations of how we communicate and present ourselves."
That is, the TV news teams have set a standard people have come to expect.
If your style of communication is drastically different from theirs, you risk
appearing unprepared, uninteresting and, worst of all, untrustworthy.
TV has rewritten the rules of public speaking. In the political realm, this
is especially vital. Whether you are in front of the House, Senate, a Gar-
den Club, or a local Rotary Club, remember that your communication is
really one-on-one. From the television, people are used to one-on-one communication. I eat breakfast with the folks on the Weather Channel every
morning. Brian Williams and Anderson Cooper are in my living room,
they talk, and I listen. They don't shout, speak in a monotone, or frown.
They don't read from a text, or at least they don't appear to. By combining*

the visual and the vocal, you set the stage for success, or what I like to call your powerful presence, which is a combination of the three main elements in this section of the book: the visual, the vocal, and the content of your message.

In this section, I will ask you to take a hard look at how others see you. How do they perceive you? First, you may make a visual assessment. Next, you may listen to the noise level in the audience and respond in a similar tone. Then, you may listen to what the audience is saying to you. How might you be able to find out what the audience is saying if you are performing on stage? Could you ask for requests or possibly research your audience before the show to see what they might be expecting? This type of role reversal, in which you visualize others, may help you to understand how others judge and perceive you.

Fortunately, it is within your means to control many of the elements with which people judge you. With each imprint, you affect individuals with whom you interact. Those people assess who you are, form opinions and judgments about you, and evaluate details that you may have over-looked. They may not realize that they are doing this, and maybe you didn't realize how much others look at you (at least not before you read this book). In any event, this is happening, either on a conscious or sub-conscious level.

Over the course of the next three chapters, you will have the oppor-tunity to gain a better understanding of the fact that how you look, how you sound, and what you say determines your success as a speaker, both in front of a large audience and in a more intimate setting. The content of your speech, the message that you are trying to get across to your audience will likely be the last thing that affects your audience, so if you can nail down the first two, the visual and the audio, then you are ahead of the game. If you can manage to hook your audience with your look and the sound of your voice, as long as you know your stuff, your message should be that much easier to communicate effectively. If you can deliver all three of these very important aspects of public speaking, then you can become a triple threat—a speaker who can master all three. You must become a triple threat to deliver your message most effectively.

First, second, and third impressions count. The following chapters will provide you with practical lessons on how to enhance your style and presence, how to master your voice, and how to speak with conviction.

3

THE LOOK

Nothing is a greater impediment to being on good terms
with others than being ill at ease with yourself.
—HONORÉ DE BALZAC

What does a rock star look like to you? Tight jeans, long hair, and
makeup? Short hair, leather, and tattoos? No matter how you picture
a rock star, what I'm talking about is something less visible but far
more important: mannerisms, body language, nonverbal behaviors,
and interaction with the audience. The common denominator all
rock stars have is a sense of coolness and collectedness that makes
them appear comfortable, believable, and interesting on the stage.
This is the rock star aura that you need to bring to the stage with you
when giving your all-important speech. Not only do you want your
speech to sound good, but you also want your audience to believe
what you say. How you carry yourself on stage will impact your audiences' reaction to you.

There are many clichés that attest to the fact that first impressions count. How many times have you heard, "You never get a second

chance to make a first impression"? Or "First impressions are lasting ones"? The fact is that all of us have a tendency to judge a book by its cover—yet another cliché—even if we shouldn't. This judgment happens quickly. Studies show that most people form a first impression of someone anywhere between seven to twenty-four seconds within first meeting that person. This means that we must be aware of the impression we are creating. When walking into a crowded room, we must command the situation before we even walk in the door. It's much easier to win over a crowd that already adores you or, at the very least, has no reason *not* to adore you.

Across the board, there are certain things that count no matter how often you're speaking or how large your audience is. Make no mistake: your appearance is what an audience or listener sees first, and it often creates the most lasting impression. Even though we know it's wrong to judge others based on their appearance, in a public speaking setting, the variables change quite a bit.

When you're speaking, you want your listener to hear what you're saying, to judge the words coming from your mouth and the ideas that those words convey. However, realistically, it is much more physical than that. Your appearance weighs much more heavily, especially in those first few moments, as your listener warms up to you, sees your physical presence, and assesses your ability to connect with him or her on some level. Listeners have a mental image of you in their minds. They see the person standing before him, and along with that image comes opinion, value, and judgment. That is how a speech becomes physical. Whether you like it or not, appearance is likely the first impression you give your audience.

Curiously enough, when focusing on delivering a message to someone, many people tend to spend most of the time developing the content of what it is they want to say: that's what they labor over, rewrite, and rethink until the moment they step in front of the audience. We work and work, and write and rewrite, and yet the audience is likely not to hear a word we say if they're too busy noticing our pants are an inch too short—let's hope not—or contemplating our natural hair color. If we want people to hear our message, it is essential that we manage our first impressions—and to do that we must be careful with our appearance and our body language.

The Halo Effect

According to a theory known as the Halo Effect, our impressions of people, and our attraction to people, deeply impact our judgment of a person's character. Knowing that now, would you take an extra fifteen minutes to evaluate yourself in a mirror before you begin an all-important presentation? The Halo Effect can work to many people's advantage, as long as they are prepared for it—conversely, the Devil Effect can be especially harmful and disadvantageous.

Have you ever met someone who always seems to catch all the breaks in life? Maybe it's a coworker who never misses a promotion, a sister or brother who always had the cutest dates, a classmate who always gets A's in class without lifting a finger, or a childhood friend who has it all. That person could be you, whether or not you realize it. What is it about these people? If you look closely enough, you may notice a glowing yellow or gold halo floating around six inches or so from the crown of their head. Don't look too hard though, or the halo might disappear. Here's why.

The halo is not really there, but it *appears* to be. Many times, bosses, suitors, teachers, or potential employers are only *seeing* their employees, dates, students, or job candidates, respectively; so it's often the image that counts. Since we were young children, our elders told us to look on the inside before making judgments about individuals' moral character, value, and self-worth. However, the research of Albert Mehrabian, professor emeritus of psychology at UCLA, who is most known for his work and publications in the 1960s on the importance of the nonverbal aspects of communications, implies that the general public only places a 7 percent emphasis on the content of a person's message. The rest comes from the aesthetic value of the individual: image and voice. This sounds preposterous, doesn't it?

My friend, I'll call her Sue, told me story about an experience she had in grad school that tests this theory. She and a friend, in their early thirties, were gaining ground in their all-important professional experience. It came to their attention how lucky they were to have landed the best jobs. One day Sue's friend asked her, "Have you ever been turned down for a job?"

Sue replied that no, she had not. Her friend thought back over her short career and realized that she hadn't either—granted this would come later, as the job market became more competitive. Regardless, they were young, and had much to learn. However, Sue asked her friend why she thought she had been so lucky. Sue knew the idea that was forming in the back of her mind before she asked the question. She was just wondering if either one of them would be bold enough to verbalize it.

Sue's friend looked at her, raised her eyebrows a bit, and scrutinized her with an inquisitive smile.

"Do you think it's because you're pretty?" Sue finally asked her friend.

"Well, it's not because I'm ugly," her friend said with a hesitant laugh. Then the friend went on to tell Sue how she believed her looks *had* played a role in getting her various jobs, even though she was extremely intelligent, well-spoken, well-read, you name it. They both knew how wrong this was, but they were convinced that it were true, that her friend's image had outplayed her character and her intellect. But it wasn't just her long, dark hair and good complexion; it was also her sense of style and the way she carried herself. Her physical appearance gave her a certain advantage over other candidates who were less aware, or less concerned with the visual.

It would not be fair to discuss how physical beauty plays a factor in the Halo Effect without deconstructing the idea of attraction altogether. Beauty is not necessarily the aesthetics of someone's physical attributes—skin, hair, eyes, nose—in this case; rather it is meant to describe how we carry ourselves as physical beings. In the case that I just cited, it was a young woman whose looks created a Halo Effect. However, I believe that the Halo Effect is just as, if not more, likely to emanate in positive ways from a strong handshake and from a strong physical presence.

Once a person's "halo" has taken effect, enter in the Rule of Connectivity, which states that the more one person feels drawn to another individual (based on that person's level of attractiveness— physical or intellectual), the more persuasive that individual becomes to the other person. The Rule of Connectivity says that there are certain elements that link two people together, a connection that occurs almost immediately. This can be a positive connection or a negative detraction. Two elements that contribute to the Rule of Connectivity are the level of attractiveness and the rate of commonalities.

In many ways, the Rule of Connectivity enables individuals to form relationships and to maintain lasting, meaningful bonds with other people. This is the case with friendships and couples. The Rule of Connectivity can also apply in less-intimate settings like public speaking events, business meetings, job interviews, or routine traffic stops. Believe it or not, you can control the Rule of Connectivity and the Halo Effect to a certain degree; if you understand that attractiveness plays into the Halo Effect and that it consists of many factors, including poise, posture, grooming, confidence, and power, then you can use the Halo Effect to play into the Rule of Connectivity.

As I stated before, there are three impressions that contribute to how others perceive us. The first is the visual; the second is the vocal; and the third is the content of our message. Even though it is the content that you probably want to focus on, think about how the visual and the vocal play into your Halo Effect and how the Rule of Connectivity may help you to establish a presence, interact with those around you, and make a difference.

Embracing Retro and Metrosexual Styles

While it's certainly true that any number of Silicon Valley millionaires seem to have an ongoing contest as to who can wear the oldest Vans and the scruffiest jeans, your best bet is to mirror Don Draper (minus the office mini-bar) of *Mad Men* for interviews, speaking engagements, and business luncheons because you can never underestimate the importance of how you look and how you dress. He is without a doubt a great example of retro-sexual and metrosexual all rolled into one.

This visual aspect is more than just making a good first impression on those around you; it is also about making yourself feel good. Make a commitment to dress the part for every event in your life, big or small. The clothing you wear can reflect your personal strength. You should wear clothes that make you feel good every day. Feeling good is a prerequisite to believing in yourself, and ultimately, if you don't believe in you, others won't believe in you.

Know your audience and dress one level up from whomever you're engaging; know that *how* you wear things is just as important as *what* you wear. No matter what, make sure your shoes are shined and of good quality. If you're on a budget, make sure that your shoes are not what you scrimp on. Be sure your belt matches and that your shirt is ironed. Nothing says success like heavy starch. Keep in mind and emulate the business traveler, explorer, or adventurer who keeps a stack of clean shirts inside his or her desk drawer. Finally, understand and accept the fact that grooming trumps style.

There is a lot to consider when evaluating your appearance in the mirror before a public speaking event. Consider this: your clothes should never be more interesting than you are. They should fit well and appear neat and clean. Clothing and how you wear it telegraphs to the world not just who you think you are, but who you want to be. Our clothes tell others about us. They can play a role in defining who we are to the public eye. Do you want others to think you're bold or self-conscious? Are you conservative? Are you creative? Are you essential, or are you an afterthought? Your attire can send all of these messages, so make your wardrobe an asset, not a liability. Remember, little things make a big difference.

In Janie Bryant's *The Fashion File: Advice, Tips, and Inspiration from the Costume Designer of Mad Men*, she offers two lists: "The Top Ten Pieces Every Woman Should Own" and "His Ten Wardrobe Essentials." Briefly summarized, women should invest in a tailored blazer, a sleek pencil skirt, a fantastic coat, a modern-day dress, a sexy cocktail dress, a classic cardigan, and a chic pair of shoes from the current season. Men should have a neutral overcoat, two suits (gray for colder months and cotton or linen for summer), one sports jacket, three dress shirts, a silk tie, one sweater, two pairs of trousers, nicely-crafted shoes (lace-up black oxfords work well with suits), and a tuxedo.

In addition to these essentials, women should have access to the following in their wardrobe:

- fabrics with texture: wool, linen, cotton
- rich colors: purple, red, blue, earth tones, skin tones
- light-colored blouses
- powder-based makeup to hide shine
- dull-finished jewelry: pearls, brushed gold or silver; and glasses with non-reflective lenses

Polish your shoes often and check the heels for wear and tear. Don't wear your nametag when you speak (I stick mine to the tablecloth. When I'm done speaking, I put it back on. The same holds true for photos (take off the nametag for the photo ops and put it back on once the picture is over). If you will often be in photographs as the only woman in the group of men, consider this when you get dressed and dress to stand out. Limit the amount of perfume you wear (if I can smell you coming or going, you have too much). Your wardrobe should help you to become just a little larger than life—and be seen as a powerful person.

Men should have access to the following in their wardrobes:

- the best suit in the room (really, guys, spend the money on one tailored suit that makes you feel like a million bucks)
- white, light blue, or blue long-sleeve shirts
- a tie and lapel that reflect the current style (no clip-on ties or suspenders)

- trouser legs that break at the front and taper down
- flat pockets, no bulging
- a tie with a simple pattern
- attractive cuff links
- long socks to cover your calves
- glasses with non-reflective lenses

Don't forget essential grooming. Shave the back of your neck. Check ears and nose for unsightly hair. Check that the tip of the tie ends at the middle of your belt (and don't use a Sharpie to hide a worn belt; for heaven's sakes, go buy a new one). Just as I suggested for women, don't wear your nametag when you speak; polish your shoes often and check the heels for wear and tear; limit the amount of aftershave or perfume you use.

As a presenter, you are always on display. If you are constantly adjusting your clothes, you will drive people nuts. If your jacket is too tight and you pull at it to give yourself space, then your audience will take note. If your tie or your collar is too tight, the audience will see that, too. So take precautions in your dress and grooming. I work with some people who believe that every day is casual Friday. No matter what your industry, do yourself a favor: clean up and be desirable.

I also have many clients who are in the political realm. Some have been in office for years. When an election rolls around and they have to campaign again, they have to buy a new suit that fits and a white or blue shirt that is not frayed at the collar or cuffs. Women may have to update a hairstyle or buy new shoes. Imagine how you would dress if you knew you might be meeting a future spouse. You would want to win that person over, wouldn't you? As a speaker that is what you are doing: trying to win over your audience.

Don't hesitate to get outside help with your look; while Internet searches can yield helpful results, sometimes the best style advice comes from an honest friend, colleague, or coach. Many people who spend a lot of time speaking in the public eye hire someone to be their image consultant. This can be helpful because you will always get an honest (but hopefully tactful) response to the question "Does this make me look fat?" If you need convincing, think of how tabloids tear celebrities apart for what they wear: it's too revealing, too ugly, too tight, too ridiculous. And these people have full-time stylists! Whether you like it or not, the people around you notice if you're having a bad hair day, if the color you're wearing doesn't suit you, or if those pants do, indeed, make you look fat. This isn't a bad thing. It means they look up to you; they want to be able to listen to what you have to say without that little voice in the back of their head commenting on the fact that you look tired or there's a spot on your shirt.

If your go-to image consultant is an unpaid friend, be sure to communicate your reason behind asking for an unbiased opinion about your look. You're not looking for flattery; you're looking for someone to give you an honest, kind assessment of your first impression. You want people who don't know you to think, "Wow, this person really has great style and knows how to dress," without dwelling too much on your clothes, hairstyle, makeup, or shoes.

Salespeople in department stores or boutiques can sometimes fill this role very well. If you're up front that you want to give them business but that you require honesty about how certain outfits fit and look on you, they will often respond truthfully but also do a lot of the picking out and pairing of outfits for you.

Sometimes I've gone so far as to ask the room service lady in my hotel room what she thinks of how I look, just to get an objective opinion. But if you find yourself stuck with no second perspective, go with your instinct. If you feel insecure in an outfit, it's going to show, no matter how much you wish you could wear it. Put it aside and wear something you know you look good and are comfortable in.

It will take some time, but once you build a good solid wardrobe, dressing for engagements will be much easier. Fashion sense can be instinctive, but it's also related to common sense, and there's a formula behind every look. Take Janie Bryant's list with you when you go shopping, and start simple. Soon enough you'll be creating your own personal style with confidence.

Body Language

As you consider how your image plays into peoples' perception of you, it's essential that you take control of your body language. What do I mean by that? I mean, "No fidgeting!" The way you carry yourself, your posture, and your bodily responses say a lot about you. Anna Lloyd Neal says, "Your poise is an outward indication of your emotional state and physical control; simply put, this means that, as a speaker, you should be in complete control of yourself in any situation." And she's right.

Avoid bobbing head syndrome. When you are listening to someone speak do not bob your head up and down like a jack-in-the-box just out of his box. That is not a position of power. I'd go so far as to say you're giving away your power if you're not in control of your body. It makes it seem as if you're willing to sell out; at the very least, it's agreement without purpose. No one is going to look to you to chart a new direction for his or her company, or follow your leadership, because your nonverbal communication says you're not in charge. They won't see a reason to listen to you or take your advice. It happens in politics and business. It happened to me when I was first elected.

I walked out of a meeting, and I overheard another attendee say, "We've got Deb's vote." I did not agree, but why did he think that? It was because of my body language. I had given a nonverbal agreement by nodding up and down. I did not intend to say that I agreed, just that I was following along. However, that speaker misinterpreted my body language, and I learned a fast lesson. What I was really thinking was, *Hurry up! Don't tell me how to build a watch; just tell me what time it is.* However, the perception was that I agreed because I was bobbing my head up and down. I had to learn to change my ways. Instead of head bobbing, try this: simply nod once or twice, slowly and with purpose. It may be the hardest thing you'll ever do. It says that you are listening, but you are not doing the head bob.

You need to maintain a calm and even delivery on the outside and the inside. Think about it next time you're sitting in a meeting and someone is drumming his fingers on the desk, shaking her leg, or simply cannot sit still. What type of impression does that person make? In public speaking, it is about control, and your physical poise is a standard by which we measure success.

Appropriate bodily action is essential to effective speaking. It helps capture and hold audience's attention and deepens the impression made by the spoken word. Conveyed properly, it adds force and conviction to your words; it can also convey meanings that you may not be able to express in words. Further, it helps to establish your own vitality. Learning to control your body language inadvertently works to relieve nervous tension. Body language can be broken down into four areas: table manners, the approach, posture, and facial expressions.

Before I begin this section, I would like for you to consider what Peggy Noonan has said in her book, *Simply Speaking*: "Some communications professionals will tell you there are specific gestures to use when you make a speech, particular ways to move your hands or use your voice. I do not think this counsel is helpful. Be yourself in your presentations, because although there have already been Vince Lombardis and Dan Rathers and Jesse Jacksons, there has never been a you before. So you might as well be you and have a good time. Authenticity isn't just half the battle, it's a real achievement." As you read the following ideas and advice on how to be a successful speaker, remember: you have to do what works for you.

Table Manners

Consider how your body language plays into what I call your table manners. Remember that the audience's impression of you comes from the visual, the vocal, and the content of your message. That said, the audience will notice your manners when you speak. Think about this, just as you learned to think about your table manners. Sit with your hands in your lap; do not put your elbows on the table; hold your fork and spoon in your right hand for eating; and transition your fork to the left and hold your knife in the right for cutting. Do these expressions sound familiar? Now, take these elements to a new context. Transpose them to the podium, or lectern.

Imagine the lectern is the dining room table at your grandmother's house for Thanksgiving Dinner. The way you position yourself at the lectern and the gestures you use will attract the audience's attention. Think about your hands and the materials on the lectern in front of you. Where is your pen? Where are your notes? Where is the microphone? How do you move your pages as you proceed through your presentation? Set guidelines and rules for yourself that show the audience that you are in control of your situation and that you are a confident speaker.

In order to convince your audience, you need to accomplish a purpose. One way to convince your audience is by using gestures: you can divide, compare, contrast, and enumerate through the use of gestures. The execution of gestures will dictate their success; they must communicate vitality. Sharp, decisive, clear gestures tell the audience that you're interested. Weak, vague, halfhearted gestures tell the audience you lack confidence in yourself.

From the minute you walk into a business meeting, pull out your chair, and sit down, people are observing you and defining their perceptions of you, as you define yourself through your actions. Most men will find a chair, sit down, cross their legs, and pull out a pen; then they will open a palm pilot, laptop, or smart phone, and rest. Women, on the other hand walk in, touch a chair, pick another one, sit down, and then dig in their purse. They often can't find what they're looking for, so they open their briefcase. Then they fluff their hair, adjust their clothes, pick imaginary lint off their shirts and skirts, fiddle with their earrings—even adjust their underclothes: pull down a slip, pull up hose—and wiggle a leg in anticipation. This list of distractions continues. These forced gestures are unnatural and appear frivolous.

Natural gestures, on the other hand, spring from inner impulse. You can gesture with one hand or both hands. Personally, I like to see people use both hands when they gesture. It gives a much larger feel and look to whatever they are emphasizing. One hand is fine, but you'll need to be careful that the one hand doesn't do the same gesture over and over.

I had a wonderful client who liked to speak from the lectern. In working with him, I noticed that he had a tendency to make an odd hand gesture with his right hand. He would extend and do a hand flip—meaning that his hand was open and equal with the floor and then suddenly he would flip it over so the inside of his hand was now open to the ceiling. When I recorded him speaking and he saw his hand just flipping back and forth, he was mortified and asked (like everyone does), "Do I do that?" (In cases such as this I'm always glad to have video footage as proof.) What I discerned was this: in his mind he thought he was gesturing out and open, but from behind the lectern it looked like a silly little hand flick, not a powerful gesture. To practice, you should video yourself and watch yourself in a mirror to see how others will see you and your gestures. Your goal is to look natural while conveying the energy and confidence you want to portray: don't become mechanical in your gestures, or it will look fake and you'll look silly.

Try these various approaches to good body language and watch yourself in the mirror as you do:

- The palm up is a standard open, friendly gesture. I encourage people to take it to the next level: spread your arms out wide with enthusiasm and show your chest.
- The palm down is universal; it slows things down and offers a quiet, calm approach.
- The vertical palm suggests division or precision.
- Point with your whole hand, not a finger or thumb. I do not allow my clients to use their index finger when they are pointing something out; it's better to use an open hand so you're not pointing anyone out. Even if you feel like nailing someone, be careful about pointing. It looks childish and

does not come off as coming from a position of strength. I have also noticed in a few recent political forums that the candidates used their thumb to point. Frankly, it looks dumb. Don't do it.

- In America, we rarely use a clenched fist, which suggests opposition, defiance, or power. (It doesn't have the same visceral image that it seems to project in other places around the world.) You can use it, but I encourage you to do so sparingly.

Your gestures need to come from your shoulder and not your elbow. When you reach to gesture, know where your hand or arm is going, and know how to bring it back. Don't fling your arm out and then drop it into place; reach it out and bring it back into place by your side in a controlled manner.

Also, think about the words you're using to describe your action and make sure your gestures mirror that description. If you're telling me you've got a big idea and your hands are four inches apart, I'm not going to understand. What you need to do is reach out wide and show me with you hands three feet apart. That's big—that's exuberance.

Most of us have two hands, and they are often the hardest things to deal with in front of an audience, so let me give you some tricks of the trade. Be careful about holding one arm. I see folks who are nervous tend to hug themselves. This is not a good use of your hands. Be careful about clasping or clutching your hands when you speak. It makes you look nervous, that or you must be rubbing lotion in. Do not do the fig leaf position; don't let your hands clasp in front of your groin area; you have nothing to hide. And for goodness sakes don't do the reverse fig leaf with your hands behind your back. Be careful about the stiff army position, whose folded arms could indicate the question, "Why am I here?" These are not personable gestures. Never lace your fingers. You are not in prayer. Try not to put your hands in your pockets. Do not play with your jewelry, and do not jingle change in your pocket.

Now here are some things that you can do: put your fist in the palm of your hand like a baseball glove; join your fingertips together and spread them out, like a steeple— this forces your arms out a little and helps you to stand up tall and take up space. These two gestures look good and will give you a sense of control, now that you know what to do with your hands.

The Approach

Now that you have established your presence on the lectern, establish your presence in the room. Before you even get to the lectern, think about *how* you are going to get to the lectern. Most of you will walk, but some of you will use wheelchairs or other devices to facilitate your journey to the podium. The presence you set forth at that moment is also a statement you make about yourself.

How you get to the lectern says a lot about you, and it may prepare the audience for what they are about to expect from you. When you initiate your approach to the podium, smile and give a half wave to the audience, if appropriate. Some people will be looking your way, and you want to acknowledge those who do. Proceed firmly and purposefully to your position in front of your audience. Take your stance in an unobtrusive way. If you are standing, be careful not to stand with your feet too far apart; it makes it hard for you to move to make a point either forward or backward.

I put my clients in what we call the runner's stance: one foot in front of the other, like you're about to take off running. This allows you step forward to your audience or step back without walking all over the place. Think of it like the ocean; it comes in and goes out fluidly, and so should your movements on the stage. Whatever you do, don't shift from side to side—you'll make your audience seasick.

Most importantly, establish good eye contact before you begin to speak. For some of you, this may come naturally. For others, it is a learned and practiced skill. Another important tip is to memorize your opening and closing lines. The reason behind this dictate is that when you reach the lectern or stage or the front of the room, you can look at your audience with confidence and begin your talk. Looking at them at the start automatically puts you in a leadership power position with your whole audience.

For some onlookers, your approach to the podium, or lectern, may be the first impression they garner from you. Consider this your grand entrance, just as you enter a crowded room at a dinner party, a business meeting, a hallway in a crowded office building, or a stage. Your game starts as soon as you take your first step, your first hop, your first roll, or your first tumble. Your image counts—so be your biggest, best self.

Think of an Olympic gymnast competing in a floor routine for the gold medal. Every step counts. Do you remember the Halo Effect? You want to produce a halo glowing six inches from the crown of your head. How do you do that? You do everything with intention. Use your power of conviction to make that halo appear. The halo creates the power of attraction, which will establish patterns of connectivity between you and your audience.

Think back to the biggest accomplishment of your life thus far. Now, imagine that your family and friends have all gathered to recognize you for this all-important accomplishment. Imagine that you are walking to the forefront of that celebration that is just for you. What will your swagger look like? How will it feel? Will it be quick paced, with a small spring to your step? Or will it be slow and deliberate? This is your million-dollar swagger. Use it whenever you walk into a room, down a hallway, across a floor, in front of an audience, or onto a stage. Applaud yourself. When you walk, keep your head up and your shoulders square. Take a peek down to your toes, then take your runner's stance.

A friend of mine told me a story that she remembered from when she was a young girl. She was walking down the hallway at school, happy to see her father who had accompanied her there; maybe it was a parent night, or back to school. She felt confident and proud to have her father with her. As she smiled at him and skipped down the hallway, he told her to put her feet forward when she walked (her toes pointed outwards slightly). She felt ashamed and embarrassed at the time, receiving his advice as a criticism. Today she says that she is grateful for his advice. She followed his suggestion and worked to correct her stance and posture. She says that today, sometimes she catches a glimpse of her toes in a mirror, and she remembers how he helped her. Take your halo, your *ruler* (of connectivity), your swagger, and these lessons with you as you step into any new speaking situation.

Posture

I don't know about your mother, but my mother always made a point of harping on my posture. She was an etiquette teacher whose only daughter was a tomboy, and she once made me walk around with books atop my head. As a public speaker, I'm forever grateful. One of the first things you need to figure out is whether or not you've got good posture and whether or not it's something you need to work on. As a coach, I sometimes want to walk up to my client, pull them up by the back of their collar, and stand them up straight and proud. Everyone responds to someone who looks powerful, and standing tall is the first step.

As important as it is to stand with power, you must also learn to sit appropriately. When it comes to sitting, sit so your backside is against the back of your chair. Now, push your shoulders back, and be sure to keep your feet flat on the floor. Adjust yourself so that your weight is evenly distributed across both hips. Your knees should be perpendicular to the floor. Next, rest your forearms on the arms of the chair and relax your shoulders without slumping.

When it comes to standing: with your heels a few inches from the base, stand with your back against a wall. Your head, shoulders, and backside should touch the flat surface. Slide one hand behind the curve of your lower back. Press your palm against the wall. If you're standing properly, the curve of your lower back should just touch the top of your hand. If it doesn't, tighten your abdominal muscles until the curve of your back touches the top of your hand. If your lower back is pressing against your hand, arch your back until it reaches the top of your hand. Note your position and adjust your posture accordingly whenever you're standing—or walking.

The great thing about good posture is that it naturally elongates your stance—this alone gives you a powerful presence. It also helps you breathe better. If you enjoy these types of exercises, you may want to consider beginning to practice yoga. Yoga can strengthen the back, shoulder, and neck muscles that are essential for good posture. It can also help you to maintain a mindful presence of your posture at all times. A dedicated yoga practice can help some individuals find the pleasure in postures and the perfect alignment that will add to their personal strength. Or you may just choose to walk around the house with a stack of books on your head.

Posture includes how you hold your head as well. Do not tilt your head to the side when you talk. Don't turn your head, but look at your audience straight on. (This is the one of the biggest issues I deal with among business folks climbing the ranks of leadership.) Many people tilt their heads out of habit. In order to break the habit, a new habit must take its place. Consider a trusted friend or coworker who can make eye contact with you and give you a signal to move your head back to straight. I also encourage you to look in a mirror and see what straight-on looks like.

A person who tilts his or her head does not command respect. Take Judge Judy, for example. You won't see her tilting her head as she reminds the defendants of the stupid choices they made that messed up their lives. Rather, she's *literally* levelheaded. The live audience and television spectators receive her message quickly—or at least before the commercial break. Holding your head level may seem trivial or insignificant, but as I said earlier, it can make or break someone's confidence in you. When your head is level, you appear powerful and are able to maintain a strong sense of presence; the whole point is that you're in position to look someone in the eye.

Your posture and how you present yourself physically make a big difference in how the audience perceives you. Stand tall and make sure that the audience can see you from the back of the room. Don't be shy. If you are smaller in stature, you may need to take a small stool to speeches so that people can see you over the podium. I'm not sure if you remember when Queen Elizabeth spoke to the US Congress; someone forgot her step stool and for the full presentation all you saw was the crown of her gray hair and not her face.

There are many postures a speaker can take at the lectern. You may have seen some of these positions during a presentation, or maybe you have taken one of them. As you read on, think about how they would look to the audience and decide for yourself if that is the image you wish to portray.

The *hugger* appears to have confronted a worst-case scenario and hugs the lectern for dear life.

The *gripper* posture—guys tend to use this one—clutches the sides of the lectern and refuses to let go to make a point.

The *leaner* cannot decide which side is comfortable so she leans from the left to the right and repeats this movement.

The *shouter*—a vocal posture—thinks the audience is deaf, so he yells to make sure that the people in the way back don't miss a word. (I don't think I am alone in suspecting that shouting is one way to cover up for a lack of good material.)

The *swayer* gently rocks from one side to the other, like a slow dance.

The *runner* is the type who paces up and down and runs around to show energy and flair. She usually loses her audience by inflicting a state of exhaustion upon them by the time the speech ends.

The *distance speaker* stands as far away from the lectern as possible, fearing the microphone or hoping not to breathe the same air as the audience.

All these odd habits will hurt you as a speaker, so remember: the lectern simply holds your notes, no more, no less. And if you feel the lectern helps you hide from your audience, be bold and step out away from it so they can see you.

Facial Expressions

Once you've nailed your approach to the podium and your posture, lighten up a bit. Keep a relaxed face, especially upon introduction.

During the first sixty seconds upon introduction and post-introduction, you should think of the calm sunlight and soft ocean breezes of the beach (or any other place that relaxes you and makes you feel peaceful); early in a speech, folks focus more so on what they see more than what they hear. Smile, lean in, and begin the process of eye contact with a few people who are nearest the stage or podium.

Eye contact is also a big part of your facial expression, and it reflects upon how your audience perceives you. Eye contact can demonstrate and help maintain a calm and even delivery. It is as important to establish eye contact as it is to keep a level head. Since our culture teaches men and women to be modest, we often avoid looking directly into another person's eyes because it may seem rude. However, if you can learn to hold someone's gaze, you gain a sense of power and forge a stronger connection.

If you have a hard time looking directly into someone's eyes, here's what to do: look at the forehead, the bridge of the nose, or the upper lip. It's called the facial triangle. If you look within these approximately four to five inches, it appears to your listener that you're looking into his or her eyes. This is good because it gives you a break so you can build up some courage to look back into that person's eyes and forge that connection. I call it the politician's gaze. (Ever wonder how they can look right at you without really seeing you?) Conversely, you can look at the right eye or left eye (and when you get the courage, you can look them eye-to-eye). What I don't want to happen is for you to *never* look at someone. People who refuse to make eye contact can appear rude or shifty, and are unable to impart the sense of intimacy and connectedness with the receiver that eye contact is able to produce. The key is to, at the very least, look like you're looking your audience in the eye.

Looking someone in the eye constantly while you're having a conversation makes a difference; the first person who turns away loses that position of power. How long should you look at someone to make good eye contact? Hold eye contact long enough for him to see that you are looking at him and seeing him. Then do your best to maintain good eye contact, and do the same with an audience of any size. And don't think for a minute you can look at the audience's hairline or just above their head.

Eye contact is a powerful ingredient of a successful delivery. Most people have a story or two to tell about establishing eye contact in various settings. The hard part may be understanding how to establish eye contact in front of a large audience. Look for a friendly or familiar face, or establish a focal point in the center of the audience and visualize the entire audience as one face. Then you can look at the nose of the audience, the forehead, or between the eyes. In doing so, your eyes may settle on a friendly listener, and if you can hold that person's gaze, you will gain a sense of power and forge a stronger connection.

When you take control of the situation through eye contact, you feel good about yourself, and that positive energy can then flow to others around you. When you feel good, your intention and your presence align with each other, and when that happens, I encourage you to smile about it. A confident, pleasant look will take you far. People will be drawn to you; you'll appear friendly, outgoing, and confident within your space. However, don't overdo it. If you smile for too long or smile too much it can create negative impression, meaning that you are overeager. Remember that your powerful presence is a combination of style and substance!

It's also important not to look too serious. It may come across as a threat to someone. When I served in my first elected position in public office, the newspaper came into our chambers to snap a candid photo. In the picture, the sides of my mouth go down. I do not naturally have a pleasant look, especially when I am thinking; my worry-line between my eyes gets deep, and the sides of my mouth turn down. My mother was the first to notice this and bring it to my attention. When she saw the photo in the newspaper, she asked, "Deb, what were you doing that made you so angry?" I explained to her that I wasn't angry, just listening intently, to which she replied, "Well, stop it." I needed a pleasant expression, like the kind I get when I think of sitting on a beach in Jamaica.

On your path to maintaining a pleasant demeanor, try these three tips:

- Press your tongue against your front teeth to lighten things and relax the muscles in your face. Your tongue pressed gently against your front teeth will give you a slight smile and help you maintain your pleasant expression. This is especially helpful if you're sitting in a conference room where everyone is deadpanned.
- Raise your eyebrows. This is the oldest trick in the book when it comes looking happy and interested.
- Record yourself, or at the very least, practice in front of mirror—but even then, what you see and what your audience sees can be very different.

Always maintain a calm and even delivery no matter what's taking place around you. Abrupt changes in your behavior could startle your audience. Act cool and in control, even if you're panicking inside. Even when you're not talking, you are still communicating, so be conscious of how you look while you're waiting or listening to someone else. Be animated and pleasant even when you're the listener. Never give the impression that you don't want to be there. By becoming comfortable with yourself and aware of the expressions on your face, you'll promote an image of confidence that people will remember and respond to.

This is important, because things will definitely go wrong, and they won't always be within your control. I once coached a client who was preparing for a mid-level presentation. I was sure that I'd nailed my goal of creating a powerful public speaker, or so it appeared. My client gave his presentation and later came to see me at my office. I got up to greet him, smiling, practicing in my head how I was going to handle the heaps of praise I was sure were coming my way.

The client was a mess. He told me he had fallen apart at the lectern. Later, I spoke to a woman who had been in the audience. She told me that the speaker was wonderful, that there had been a slight technical problem with the microphone, but they fixed it and the presentation went on. When I relayed this information back to my client, he was reassured. Looking back at the presentation, he realized that even though he had been feeling unsure on the inside and the problem with the microphone had put him on edge, he remembered what we had discussed in training. He kept his head up high and his voice steady, and in doing so, he had maintained his poise and composure. For that, he thanked me—and he realized something valuable. No matter how you're feeling inside, it's what you're showing on the outside that counts.

Your look is the foundation of your powerful presence. It's the first thing you should focus on defining and honing so that it represents your passion and your professionalism. No one creates a look overnight so don't get overwhelmed. Rather, take it one step at a time, slowly building your wardrobe and practicing your posture, facial expressions, and eye contact every day. A positive first impression will make people want to stick around for their second impression: your voice.

4

THE VOICE

Words mean more than what is set down on paper. It takes the human voice to infuse them with shades of deeper meaning.
—MAYA ANGELOU

You are a rock star. Not only do you want your audience to enjoy the show, but you also want them to buy your music after the show has ended. You want them to believe what you say and believe in your vision. In this regard, believe it or not, the sound of your voice is likely more important in the delivery of your message and how your listener receives that message than what you're actually saying.

Voice is the second component of powerful presence, and it speaks volumes about your confidence. It is a part of your unique thumbprint, your personal signature, and it conveys your level of interest, enthusiasm, and energy. With increased focus on your vocal power, you will gain insight into how well you execute diction and how you can increase your vocal clarity.

I know a woman who teaches French as a foreign language to various ages of students, from elementary through university. One of the predominant methodologies that she applies to teaching a foreign language is to use the immersion approach, which is to stay in the foreign, or target, language one hundred percent of the class time. Research has proven that immersion is the most effective way to learn a language. That might sound frustrating or intimidating, but think about how you learned your original language. It was a type of immersion, wasn't it? Well, just as your caregivers did for you, this teacher uses hand gestures, props, and intonation, among a variety of other things, to get her students motivated and to increase their comprehension of the French language. The most interesting part is that the students understand and can respond in French, even though they don't understand much of what she is saying. This teacher employs her voice as a tool to assist her students' comprehension of a foreign language.

Essentially, this is what is happening during the first few moments of your speech, when your image and the sound of your voice are registering on your audience. They are not really hearing *what* you are saying. They are assessing your image and the sound of your voice. The enthusiasm, tonal variations, and intonation are all elements of your vocal communication skills and they factor into your power of conviction and your powerful presence. This assessment is likely to occur whether the listener knows it or not, although if your voice has a particularly positive or negative impact, it can become obvious to the listener, just like with your look. Maybe there's something about the sound that reminds the listener of something unpleasant, or conversely, maybe your voice is full of intonation and enthusiasm and as a result that enthusiasm affects the listener in a positive way.

Vocal Production and Power

Your voice is an amazing instrument. The sound and depth of it depend greatly on your lips, tongue, teeth, jaw, the opening up and stretching of your mouth, your diaphragm, your core stomach muscles, and how you're able to dip into what's just beyond your rib cage. You should also be able to judge the inherent value of your voice and where you need to up the ante. Here's a hint to start: you will *always* need a microphone. This is the first step to speaking with power and making sure your voice conveys authority. Once you understand the value of a powerful voice—and learn to use it—you will be amazed at the response from others.

There are three standard textbook discussions for your voice. Phonation is the sound of your voice. Resonation is the loudness of your voice. Articulation is the distinct sounds your voice makes (it's what makes you, well, you) by the working of your teeth, tongue, lips, and jaw. This is why you need to see your mouth in a mirror when you speak. You must be able to assess how you form words to assess how you speak. I use a recorder or video camera for my clients. Inevitability they'll ask, "Do I really sound like that?" It often comes as a shock—how we think we sound (what we hear) and how we actually sound are very different.

For some people, trying to grasp the idea of their own vocal production is like learning a foreign language. Maybe you struggle to hear the intonation in your voice, or maybe this comes naturally. Regardless of which camp you fall into, there are some training techniques you can use to help. Imagine your life as an opera singer and consider the intense training that must accompany such a career. Imagine who your voice coach or teacher may be. What would their role be in helping you to achieve your best performance? Maybe you would train with your coach for several months before a big performance. During your training sessions, you might try different voice drills and projection techniques. Your life as an opera singer would rest on the sound of your voice. Your income, your stress, your success, and your reputation would depend on how well you project and train your voice.

Now step back into your own shoes. Picture yourself standing in front of your target audience, and think like an opera singer. The first step is to focus on your breath. We all know that a deep, strong breath will help calm you down and give your lungs a chance to expand and fill with air, but it will also help you speak with power. When you don't breathe properly, it will harm your speaking voice in the long run and just might turn off your audience due to your weak voice.

There are three ways to breathe, but for our purposes here I want to focus on the two most common: clavicle and diaphragmatic breathing. Clavicle breathing is known as shallow breathing. This occurs when you're running or doing something strenuous and need to fill your lungs with air quickly. The air is brought in through the chest cavity, and your shoulders rise and fall with each breath—not great for your health or for long periods of time, as you need to get the oxygen into your system to help your heart and brain and other organs breathe. When you start speaking, sometimes you will feel like this is happening; if so, stop and breathe deeply to put yourself in your proper vocal range. Epigastric breathing, more commonly known as breathing from your diaphragm, is the best for speakers and singers who need to hold strong and steady through a performance. It's also much better for the body. Practicing deep breaths will calm you down and give you the voice power you need to start strong and stay strong. It will also smooth your voice. You will know you're doing diaphragmatic breathing when you sing and can hold a note for a relatively long period of time (let's say twelve to fifteen seconds). This is also when your stomach, rather than your chest, rises and falls with air intake.

Now that you can breathe—and speak—let's consider the volume of your voice, the force of your voice, and the rate of utterance or speed of your speaking. Your voice comes from your core. That's why even physically small folks can have booming voices and giants can sound small.

When my clients ask how to develop a stronger voice, I often find they need to return to childhood. It's ingrained in some people to speak softly. As children, many of us took it to heart when our parents and teachers told us to use our inside voices, to not interrupt adults when they were talking, or even that children should be seen and not heard. We carried these limitations into adulthood, and they are now working against us in the business world. You *do* have a voice, and you *should* be heard. It is absolutely possible to change those old habits and learn to speak with volume, so confront these limiting beliefs and speak to be heard.

The force of your voice is measured by how loud you can be without straining. To be forceful, you will need to get your breathing under control so you have the air to hold your power. The pitch of your voice—the sound of it—is something else you should understand. Do you have a high pitch or low pitch? Most folks are happy with their pitch because it sounds natural to them (even if it's squeaky), but by working with a vocal coach, you can change the pitch of your voice. Also, keep in mind that just because you might have an unusual voice doesn't mean that you automatically have a negative impact on your audience. For instance, I don't mind a deep, raspy voice. My favorite voice was Suzanne Pleshette from *The Bob Newhart Show*, and as she aged her smoker's voice was very distinct and sexy (though this is not an endorsement to get you to start smoking!).

Another element to consider is your rate of utterance or how fast you speak. It's never a good idea to speak too fast—your listeners will not be able to understand what you say, and if they're taking notes, they'll be rushed and have trouble focusing. However, you don't want to speak too slowly, either. I'm from the South, and we tend to speak more slowly down here; we're not in that much of a hurry. When I go above the Mason-Dixon Line to train or speak at a conference, I catch myself speeding up. Of course, in any big city everything moves more quickly, including speaking rate, but this isn't always the best rule of thumb when you're speaking. Speaking too quickly can give the impression that you're afraid people won't stick around to listen to what you say. When you are confident that what you're saying is relevant and interesting, you can speak more slowly and even pause for effect.

Speaking of the Mason-Dixon Line, accents are another thing to be considered. If you come from a part of the United States or the world that flavors your voice, this can be used to your advantage, but it can also detract from your message. Accents can be used to create your persona as a speaker—a slightly exotic foreign accent, a charming Southern one, a funny or sarcastic northeastern one, etc. But of utmost importance is being understood. I had a wonderful client who hailed from China, and although everyone who heard her speak in private conversations could understand her accent, when she started speaking more in the community, I could see that we needed to open her presentation with a line or two that would help tune listeners' ears to her subtle accent.

The takeaway here is that you aren't stuck with the voice you have. Whether you have a rushed voice, a quiet voice, or a voice with an accent, at any time and any age, with practice you can change the voice you have to the one you want.

Vocal Inflection: Fusing Language and Voice

The excitement and energy that you put into a presentation will bring a return on your investment. Speaking with excitement, energy, and power will set you apart, and your audience will remember you—not just what you say, but how you say it. Be sure to get enough mental and physical rest before a presentation, but if you do end up exhausted, skip it. You will not be at your best, and it will show. If you deliver a bad presentation, you may never get another chance to make your pitch.

If you are monotone, you'll be dead in the water and no one will listen, so vary your voice. You do this when you read children's stories. Think about it: no one reads *The Cat in the Hat* like a budget report. No, you hit the highs and lows with your voice with energy and, if you're doing it right, enthusiasm. If I'm telling a big story, my voice goes up and is full. If I'm telling a serious story, my voice will drop and be more distinctive. I may even whisper or pause to get my point across. If I'm angry, I'll raise my voice or drop it down. Vary your voice to give more meaning to what you say. Remember to be careful about letting your voice rise at the end of a sentence; it sounds like you're asking a question rather than making a statement. Don't drop off at the end of your sentence; maintain a powerful voice until the end or take a breath to carry you there.

Did you know that the lower your voice, the more credible you sound? Think of all the television and radio commercials that feature low-voiced men and women. If you hear your voice starting to rise, stop and take a breath. It will put you automatically back in your vocal range.

A lower voice also conveys a position of power, which people listen and respond to. Start each new thought with a new breath of air to begin with power, and save enough breath, or take another, to end with power. If you need more force, or need to enhance your ability to be in command of a situation, stand up when you speak. It will help extra air and energy come through in your voice. Good speakers develop a rhythm to their pace and a tone that defines their speaking voice.

In campaign settings, I have often see a sign above the telephone bank that says, "Keep smiling while dialing; it will show in your voice." It really does. This may explain why some people bought magazine subscriptions to the year 2020—someone was smiling on the other end of the line.

When you speak, keep your voice level and strong. Be bold in your posture, language, and volume. A soft, sweet, or reassuring voice may be fine in the home environment, but it is not the best way to be perceived in today's culture of power. How many times have you had a great idea but didn't push it, just made an off-the-cuff remark, and someone else heard your idea, said the same thing out loud, and took control of it? That person gets the recognition and acclaim for your idea. Take ownership of what you are saying. When you speak, speak with the power of conviction, and speak loudly enough so that others can hear you. Most people do not speak out loud because they're afraid of being wrong and being mocked or criticized by others. However, it's much more unfortunate to let an opportunity go by because you're afraid of being embarrassed or laughed at. Don't be silenced by the fear of saying the wrong thing. Most opportunities are not a single shot. We usually have an opportunity to go back and correct mistakes. If you have developed a personality of strength and power, you will be able to laugh at your mistakes and move forward. Do not consider your mistakes as failure; they are an opportunity to regroup and reconsider thoughts and actions so that you can learn to do better next time.

The Right to Speak

It's one thing to speak, and it's another thing to be heard. Ideally, a combination of the two will take place, which is the best possible combination. If you can bridge the two aspects of language, meaning that when you speak, people listen, and they hear what you are saying, then you are creating a powerful vocal presence.

When it comes to speaking powerfully and being heard, there are two bad habits you should always avoid: asking for permission to speak, and apologizing to be polite. These are two of the most annoying habits in the world, and if you use them, they are harming your image. You do not have to ask permission to speak, nor should you apologize for things you have no control over.

I have a friend who has the first of these bad habits—she is always asking, "Can I ask you a question?" In all the years I've known her, I've never heard anyone say to her, "No, you can't ask me," which underlines the point that asking is unnecessary and redundant. Business professionals do not ask to speak because it puts them at a disadvantage.

Phrases like these are crutches that I believe come from a deep-seated belief of unimportance. You don't need an excuse to say what you want to say. When you ask for one, you diminish the fact that you have a position of power. Drop "I'm sorry" from your public speaking and business vocabulary. Do not apologize unless you are wrong. Stop saying you're sorry just to be polite. Instead of saying you're sorry, learn to say, "Pardon me," and "Excuse me." In other words, learn to speak powerfully—learn to choose words that mean what you want to say. Find a balance and train yourself to speak with intention and power, loudly enough to be heard and forcefully enough to be listened to.

When you lose the right to speak, your audience no longer hears you and your credibility is at risk. Do not let others interrupt you. Finish what you are saying, and don't let others complete your sentences. When you complete anything, even a spoken sentence, you boost your self-esteem. You need to be able to complete your thoughts. How many times have you begun to explain a position when out of nowhere someone cuts you off and begins a conversation like you never existed or were even speaking? Out of politeness or sheer shock, the others at the table don't know where to look. If someone is cutting you off in conversation, try this:

- Increase the volume of your voice as you continue talking. Gently become louder so the person knows you're not done yet.
- Hold up your index finger (like my hero, Judge Judy). It's sort of like a yield sign to the clueless.
- If that does not work, simply say out loud, "Hold it, and let me finish this thought."

The first time you do this people may be shocked by your boldness, but rest assured that after your listener learns that you have a right to speak, he or she may interrupt less. I learned this at an early age. My brothers did this to me all the time until my dad finally told me not to stop talking or I would keep getting cut off. Soon enough, they learned to let me finish what I was saying. Even if you think you can't do this, trust me and try it anyway. You'll be amazed by how it will change your position of power.

There are a number of other tips to avoid being interrupted or losing your audience's interest. Always get to the point fast. Don't waste ten minutes of your twenty-minute presentation talking background. Be specific to your point, not to everything; if listeners want to know more, they will ask. Remember that for most people, time is money, so do everyone a favor and just cut to the chase. Never start a statement with the phrase, "I don't know." Say, "I'll check on that," "I'll get back to you," or "That's an interesting thought."

Women especially need to take note of this. Deborah Tannen, a linguist at Georgetown University, has documented the speech patterns of women. She notes, "Throughout history women have listened more than they've spoken and agreed more than they have confronted. They have been delicate and indirect in their word choices, which make them sound like they are confused...unsure... and uncommitted."

Don't let this be you. There are many wonderful things about being a woman, but being quiet is not one of them. Especially if you are making your living speaking or your job requires that you engage to be seen as credible, you must get over fears of being thought "unladylike," "bitchy," or "bossy." This does not mean you need to be vulgar or rude. Rather, use your calm but powerful voice to be heard using the techniques in this chapter, and watch how people's response to your changes.

The power of your voice cannot be underestimated. If your look gives a positive first impression, it's absolutely essential that you back it up with a confident, evenly pitched, energetic voice. Record yourself and listen to how *what* you say is affected by *how* you say it—your inflection, breathing, and force. Watch yourself in the mirror so you can see how your facial expressions affect your tone, and vice versa. With practice, your new, powerful voice will become second nature, and your listeners will sit up and take notice.

5

THE CONTENT

I've learned that people will forget what you said, people forget what you did, but people will never forget how you made them feel.
—MAYA ANGELOU

Once your look and your voice are top-notch, it's time to move on to your audience's favorite part of your presentation: the content. When combined with your appearance and your voice, and your content must be top-notch; altogether this "powerful presence" must portray the single best image of yourself that you can convey. Remember, you want to be a rock star. You want to speak in front of an audience without fear. Combining the triple threat of your image, your voice, and your message ensures that the next time you stand up in front of an audience, you can do so with confidence.

There are three aspects to content: researching, organizing, and writing an impactful speech, all of which are as important as your execution. Each extension—how you control your voice, how you carry yourself, and what you say—is vital because you now know that people register more of what they see than what they hear. However, hearing is what pulls it all together. Without belittling the seemingly superficial importance I've already placed on looking and sounding the part, you need to craft your message very carefully. You will never deliver a life-changing message, or redirect a thought, if you fail to meaningfully craft your content.

Look at it this way: no one is going to buy a farm, a house, or a piece of property based purely on rumor or curb appeal. In fact, I'd much rather hear an audience member say, "Well, she could have made better eye contact" or "She needed to speak into the microphone" than "Wow, she was all over the map" or "It's obvious that she had no idea what she was talking about." If your message is worth saying, it's worth saying well. Make no mistake: even if you have the perfect stance and the inimitable well-paced vocal pauses of Ronald Reagan, if the content of your presentation is jumbled, incoherent, and unorganized, you will have failed.

Looking and sounding good convinces people to stick around to hear what you have to say. It gives you the confidence to say it well. But it is *having quality content* that keeps people coming back for more, time and time again. It's *content* that changes the way people think at the end of the day. It's *content* that opens up avenues of possibility in your listeners' thoughts, careers, and lives, and in your life and career as a speaker and businessperson. While looking good and sounding good create opportunity, I am convinced that *content* is one of the surest ways to win over an audience.

So, how do you put this information together to create the no-fear public speaker who can perform on stage like a rock star? The question is not only how to put it all together but also how to achieve the greatest impact during the time that you hold your audience's attention. Always remember to start with your core theme. In doing so, give your audience a glimpse of what it is that you hope to share with them during your presentation. Think of it as a spoiler, if you will, to a book or a movie. This will only work once you know exactly what it is you want to say. This will also enable you to come full circle by the end of your speech. So, the essential reminder here is: know exactly what you want to say.

Once you have your idea framed in your mind. Go about explaining it in a logical and well-organized manner. Remember to be a good storyteller. Most people enjoy listening to stories. It's a common element in most cultures and a favored pastime. What is the most important thing that you need to say to your group during your speech? Take time leading up to it and think about why they need to hear it. Find a word, a phrase, or a well-known quote and keep it in the forefront as you begin to develop your presentation. Your theme matters because it's the glue that holds your talk together. Don't lose sight of the topic or theme in the midst of all the great facts and figures and stories and quotes. Your theme matters. Always keep it loud and at the forefront of your speech.

Once you've committed to your theme, craft *your* stories (not someone else's). Dig deep to find stories that reflect an incident or event that changed you in some way and had a great impact on your life (or, when appropriate and necessary, the life of someone else). Your intent is to share that impact with your audience. Think about how this story changed you, why it changed you, and if it had not happened, how would you be different today. And then craft that story down to about forty-five seconds to one minute. This will take some time but it is worth it because although I preach that your stories are key, they simply are dropped into you message to keep your audience in sync with you as you lead them through your topic. Your stories give a glimpse of who you are and what drives you. Your audience needs to see and feel that energy to learn.

Next, make sure that you've thoroughly researched and are ready to add in your facts. You need to be able to stand firmly on what you're teaching, speaking about, and campaigning. Your facts need to be relevant and true. Everything you say will be questioned, so make sure you're in the right. And remember you can, and should, always give yourself some leeway by using words that give you "cover." That means, as often as necessary, use words like: generally, usually, and normally. These words will help to keep you safe from an audience member who may disagree with you. (We'll go into further detail on this in Chapter Seven: The Performance.)

Then remember this line: *people remember how you make them feel more than what you say.* I repeat this often because it's true. You want your audience to feel good. This is why you want to connect with your audience. Your message might not be able to do that alone, so if possible, try some humor. When attempting a new joke, it's always best to try it out with a few people before doing so in front of a large audience. Gauge the response of your sample audience. If it works for them, it is likely to work for others. Never use comedy directed at other people. It may harm them in an unknown way and you may never get a chance to take that back.

If you do decide to add humor to part of the presentation, slow down and laugh out loud with the audience so the lines of communication are open wide. Do not leave room for misinterpretation. It is true that a comedic approach can take some practice, but don't let that discourage you. Humor is essential in today's serious world. Yes, you will still be considered a serious person even if you tell a funny story or two. Just keep it tasteful and within the boundaries that are set by your audience and it will add a pleasant dimension to you and your topic. If stories about you and your crazy family are not on the table for discussion, listen to the late night comedians, or read a family-friendly magazine like readers digest that has plenty of good material for you to use. As always, if you are going to borrow someone else's material, be sure to reference the source in your speech.

Every Audience Participates

Before you accept an invitation to speak or present, it's important to know your audience. Check with the meeting planner or the person who invited you to speak and ask them to give you goals or objectives for the event so you both will be successful. Determine a general age group, or generation, that makes up your potential audience. Why is this important? Older individuals have more experiences on which to base their judgments; they have more years of routines and habits that may be more difficult to change. Play upon their experiences, work at creating your halo, and finesse the application of the Rule of Connectivity. Did you know that, traditionally, younger people tend to be less critical of information than older people are? And they will tweet your message if they find value. They seem to be more open to new ideas, but to reach them they need to hear energy in your voice and delivery. Find a way for your audience to connect with you.

While age and the ability to absorb the information matters, so does the time, place, and expected manner of the speech. The assessment of your audience is no different from what they will be doing to you. Your job is just harder because you may have hundreds of people to consider. As a template, here are several questions you should ask yourself to insure that your speech is appropriate:

- Why is the audience coming to see me speak?
- Are there particular topics and issues I must address? Is there a specific topic I've been asked to present?

- Why was I asked to speak?
- Am I on a panel, or a member of a working group?
- What's the expectation of my participation?
- What's the expected manner of the speech?
- Is the audience coming to support me or fight me? Will the audience question me, or will they be more apt to get on board with my campaign?
- What does the audience expect to learn or take away from my presentation?
- What's their attitude toward the subject or their position on the issue?
- What are the audience's general demographics? What are their occupations and education?
- Am I expected to be teaching or cheerleading? Am I considered the information guru or the entertaining speaker?

Once you've determined the demographics of your audience, think about planning an appropriate presentation that will sell your vision to that particular group. Think about the big picture. First, where will you be speaking? In an auditorium, at a hotel ballroom, in an office setting? Not only do you need to know where you'll be speaking, but you must also think about *when* you'll be speaking. If the event is first thing in morning, you'll definitely want to bring energy—for me it's a caffeine-fueled high. If it's a dinner event, you should aim to be especially funny, as your audience most likely has had a long day—they don't want to be taught, they want to be entertained. Think about location, time of event, and what's needed from you to perform.

Always check with the event or meeting planner to make certain you are clearly informed on the goals or objectives for the event. Never walk in unprepared. If you have a question about your location or topic or expectation, you have the right to call the person who asked you to speak and run down the guidelines as to what they're hoping to accomplish by having you. Always research the organization to know who they are; a well-paid compliment to their organization will be a feather in your cap, just as calling the organization by the wrong name will kill your message. It's amazing to me when speakers show up without knowing to whom they will be speaking. And I will add that you probably want to Google the group to see if there is any news about them online or in print. I live by the adage, "It's better to know who I'm speaking to rather than to be spoken about." Above all, your goal should be to get to know your audience in a way that you can motivate them to want to learn more about whatever it is you have to say.

Before you begin crafting any presentation, take five minutes to:

- Understand what you want your audience to take away.
- Work at being able to sum up your message in a few words.
- Be able to articulate the mission statement or the meat of your message.

It's a Small World

Once you've considered and reconsidered your main objective, it's best to think about everything else in degrees. Similar to the trivia game Six Degrees of Kevin Bacon (which rests on an assumption that anyone involved in the Hollywood film industry can be linked to actor Kevin Bacon within six steps), the concept of the *small world phenomenon* is a cornerstone of crafting a speech.

In the trivia game there's something that's called the Bacon number. An actor's Bacon number is the number of degrees he or she is from Kevin Bacon. For example, Meryl Streep's number is one, because she was actually in the movie *The River Wild* with Kevin Bacon. John Travolta has a Kevin Bacon number of two; he was never actually in a movie with Kevin Bacon, but he was in a short film with John Legend, who starred in the movie *Loverboy*, which Kevin Bacon directed.

This trivia game is a modern-day application of the Erd?s number. The Erd?s number describes the "collaborative distance" between a person and the mathematician Paul Erd?s, one of the most prolific modern writers of mathematical papers. Twenty-five years before the Bacon number became part of America's culture, the Erd?s number was created as a tribute and rather cheeky measurement of one's mathematical prominence.

Let's consider what collaborative distance means. As a speaker, it is important to be aware of the shortest path to reaching your audience. This doesn't mean that you will fail or succeed, only that the cards may or may not be stacked in your favor. Not enjoying a relatively close collaborative distance with your audience *does not* mean certain failure; it just means that you, as the speaker, will have to work a little harder to help your audience narrow the gap. On the same hand, enjoying a relatively close collaborative distance does not mean certain success, only that you, as the speaker, may not need to work as hard to narrow the gap.

When I was new to politics—before I'd even held a public office— I worked for years as a scheduler, campaign manager, finance chair, speechwriter, and most every job in between. And although I'd yet to win an election, I still had the good fortune of being asked to speak at conferences about the new trends in campaign speeches. Some of my first audiences were elected women, and while they appreciated my knowledge, I was at a disadvantage since I'd never actually won an election. In these instances my collaborative distance was good but not great; I hadn't truly walked in my audience's shoes. Once I'd won an election, quite suddenly, I closed the gap on the collaborative distance for those speaking engagements.

It's not an exact science. It's a matter of finding the degree of collaborative distance and meeting your audience somewhere in the middle. Give them a little ground, and they'll return the favor by being attentive. Don't think you'll always have the support of every single audience member, but crafting a speech that's meaningful and self-aware should be a point of departure.

Take everything except for the speech, lecture, or presentation off the table for a minute and jot down the answers to these questions. Make a note of any other questions that may arise.

- Do you know the collaborative distance between you and your audience?
- If you're looking at the theme of your speech, is the general topic about which you are speaking something that your audience is familiar with?
- How familiar are you with the subject?
- Are you the expert?
- Is your message general or is it polarizing?
- Is it polemic or is it unbiased?
- How passionate are you about your subject?
- How familiar are you with your subject?
- If you're at all acquainted with your audience, how passionate do you suspect they are about your subject?
- In a similar vein, how familiar do you suspect your audience is with your topic?

Even if it's something your audience won't necessarily initially care about or may be downright against, you'll want to relate to their needs and experiences. For instance, imagine that you are speaking to a group of workers who've always done things a certain way. Their company is about to roll out a whole new set of protocols, and the workers are nervous about the big change. Begin your speech with an anecdote about something very difficult that you overcame, or choose a national hero who struggled in the same way, and you might decrease your collaborative distance. In no way will a lack or an excess of collaborative distance make or break your lecture or presentation, but it will give insight on how you should approach the crafting of your presentation.

Content Is King

The first thing you should consider when writing your speech is that in addition to conveying information, a speech must entertain or move people to action. Your goal is to make your listeners think, care, respond, and act. Find a unifying theme. This will help you organize the speech logically. Develop one or two good quotes, stories, and analogies, especially G-rated personal anecdotes. Insert them early in the speech and develop the central message from the opening.

If your jokes are old, your stories are someone else's stories (and not offered as such), or your facts are dated or untrue, then your audience will not trust you, and they are unlikely to forgive and forget easily. The absolute best way I know to ensure a long life in public speaking is to say things that people *should* hear. The trick is to arouse listener curiosity and have a single concept in mind with a clear, concise message that contains no more than three key points and a definite ending.

Also consider whether there are there particular topics that you must address. If so, what are they? Nothing is worse than to have a great title to your presentation and a lousy speech. I often work with political candidates, and many times I will ask them to stand and say, "This campaign is about crime, education, and taxes, but in our time here together for today, let me focus on education." Why do I have them do that? It's because I want the audience to know that my candidate has a big view, but he or she won't or can't tell you everything in one sitting. You will have to follow the candidate or the campaign, or go to another neighborhood coffee shop to hear the rest of the story. This is relevant in business, as well. Often we don't have enough time to delve into every aspect of our industry, but we can say, "Our company's focus will be on x, y, and z, but today let's discuss z."

As a speech trainer, I make my clients write out their presentations. When crafting yours, you'll need to write it out, then cull it, tighten it, and find the right cadence for your message. There are three general rules to remember while drafting your speech and making decisions about its content.

First, be accurate and clear. There's little doubt that your audience will quickly tweet your mistakes, so be sure of your facts. Make certain you know enough about the facts or issues to define your topic clearly. It's imperative that you know what you're talking about, so take the time to learn your topic before you arrive for your presentation. Above all, be careful that your interpretation of the facts are founded and can be easily substantiated. Manipulating the facts to support an unfounded position can often lead to embarrassment, undesired scrutiny, and a loss of respect. Also, using language that's current, professional, and vivid will help reduce the risk of being misunderstood and will ensure your message comes across as clear as possible.

Next, maintain a level of impartiality. I know this may seem odd, but unless you're paid to persuade an audience to come over to your side, try to stick to the middle or you'll offend the majority and never be invited back. Now, if it's something you're willing to fall on your sword for, then all the more power to you, but I see and hear speakers get into verbal fisticuffs all the time to prove a point that doesn't matter. Don't be influenced by prejudices. Don't deal in generalities. When necessary, have at the very least a basic understanding of different viewpoints.

Lastly, be interesting. If you want to be invited back, be thought provoking. It's your responsibility to entertain, educate, or influence your audience. And remember, just because it's interesting to you doesn't mean it will interest your audience. We've all been cornered by a new parent dying to tell us the latest "hilarious" thing junior has done, only to be stuck in a one-sided, hour-long conversation that, truthfully, we could have done without. If you know your audience, you'll be less likely to be standing on the stage laughing at your own jokes.

When it comes to the content of your speech, remember your vision and remember to appeal to your audience. Although you want your speech to be an accurate representation of the naturally, spontaneously spoken word, don't overlook the fact that it takes careful planning. Assess your audience, plan your topic, decide what type of speech it will be, and define your purpose. When you begin writing your speech, understand it as an essay. An essay is meant to touch a chord, ring a bell, punch a button, sing a song, or paint a picture. It's persuasive and deals with something that is meaningful to the reader or listener. Outline your speech as an essay first, point by point, and then flesh it out with short, crisp sentences that make your case.

When you begin to choose, arrange, and craft your content, it's the message, the lessons, and the stories that should stand on their own. Think of it as your presentation's mission statement. Ultimately, however, before you even sit down to organize your presentation, think about what you want your audience to remember or know. In the hour you have of their time, what do you want your audience to be able to repeat to someone else after your presentation? What are they supposed to take away at the end of that hour? Once you have the end goal in mind, you can begin.

This is backwards planning, and it's very effective, especially if you have trouble knowing where to start. First things first, your end destination is often the place to start. Begin with the end in mind. If you put your closing remarks first, you'll blow away the competition. Let's say you're giving a talk on why your community should fund a non-kill animal shelter. What's the last thing you want to say to your audience? Start there. Because your audience doesn't have the time or the interest for you to build to your "boom," just get there quickly and grab them so they will want to hear the build-up and how you got there.

In addition to beginning with the end, you also want to begin with style. A jolt of action, humor, or tension is a fantastic way to grab an audience from the get-go. That said, if you decide to start with a story, you'll really need to consider your audience, their age, and whether or not the story is genuinely compelling. I can tell you after years of speaking that nothing pulls an audience in like an unpredictable personal story or an issue you have dealt with personally; just make sure you have an outcome that is relevant to the audience.

One way to begin with the end and capture the audience immediately is to make a big fat claim. I've been teaching this for a while because it's a great way to quickly state your case. It works like this: write down your claim to fame, what makes you a rock star, or what makes you so amazing that anyone should listen to you. My big fat claim is that I can add an extra zero to your income. That's a big promise and a way to reel my audience in. It makes them want to listen to every detail of my speech. Then I explain that as an executive speech and presentation coach, I can help you craft a message your audience will listen to, hear, and take action on.

A working example of big fat claim comes from a client I had last year. My client is the president of a major retailing firm. During the holiday season, due to circumstances beyond his control, a major shipment was stuck at sea and unable to dock. Stock prices plummeted, which left shareholders not feeling at all festive—or forgiving. As we worked through the presentation he was due to give at the annual shareholder meeting, he was adamant that we not speak about the stock. I told him there were no two ways about it: he had to confront the issue up front. It took persuading, but he finally acquiesced. At the very start of his presentation, he stopped, looked at the group, and said, "Many of you are wondering what's happened to our stock. Let me explain." By the time he was done speaking, he'd received the longest applause he'd ever gotten, and there were no questions from the audience.

Brevity and Levity

It's a fact that the average sound bite in 1968 was 42.3 seconds. In 1988 it was 9.8 seconds; in 1992, it was 7.3 seconds; and in 2006, it was 4.5 seconds. My point is: be brief. Our culture is one of fast food, speed dating, and instant gratification. We want what we want, and we want it now. So don't keep your audience waiting!

Now that you've considered your topic and your audience, you'll want to start writing your actual speech. In order to do that, you'll need to know how long it should be. This depends on a number of factors, but keep this in mind: the latest studies show that the attention span of today's audience is about one thousand seconds, or sixteen and a half minutes. Last time I checked it had dropped to fifteen minutes and likely continues to drop on a regular basis.

Because of this, one of the most important things to remember when choosing your content is to keep your presentation short (unless your audience is forewarned that it'll be a two-hour tour, or they've paid to be there and they want your autograph). Ask yourself about the length of time you intend to speak. Have you timed yourself? In general, a seven-page double-spaced paper should take approximately twenty minutes to read, without improvisation. People will excuse all kinds of lousy speechmaking, but nobody forgives the pain of a long speech. Twenty-five to thirty minutes is a long speech, fifteen to twenty minutes is a medium-long speech, and seven to ten minutes is a nice short speech. The ideal time is twelve minutes.

Beyond that it's a matter of being relevant, knowledgeable about your subject, making folks laugh, and offering a blend of insight, humility, personal or community benefit, and content that inspires others.

The Art of Storytelling

Garrison Keillor, host of the NPR radio show *A Prairie Home Companion* since 1974, reminisced, "You get older, and you realize there are no answers, just stories." Stories teach us what's important—and what's not important. They teach us what's real as well as what's possible. Stories get us to dream, appreciate, understand, commiserate, or be cautious—sometimes they do any number of these in tandem.

Stories can be kindling and fuel to a fire, or they can be a wet blanket. They offer clarity. They bring up new questions. They offer new horizons.

We've been telling stories since time began. I grew up with *One Thousand and One Nights*, a collection of Middle Eastern and South Asian stories and folktales compiled in Arabic during the Islamic Golden Age. You may have known it as *Arabian Nights* from the first English translation. The work was collected over many centuries by various authors, translators, and scholars across the Middle East, Central Asia, and North Africa. The tales themselves trace their roots back to ancient and medieval Arabic, Persian, Indian, Turkish, Egyptian, and Mesopotamian folklore and literature.

One of the featured stories retells an account of a Persian king and his new bride. Upon discovering his new wife's infidelity, King Shahryar (sha-har-ray-ard) has her executed and then declares all women to be unfaithful. He begins to marry a succession of women only to execute each one the following morning. Eventually the vizier, whose duty it is to provide the women, cannot find any more. Scheherazade (sha-hair-ra-zad), the vizier's daughter, offers herself as the next bride, and her father reluctantly agrees. On the night of their marriage, Scheherazade begins to tell the king a tale, but it doesn't end. The king is forced to postpone her execution in order to hear the conclusion. The next night, as soon as she finishes the tale, she begins a new one, and the king, eager to hear the conclusion, postpones her execution yet again. So it goes on for one thousand and one nights.

Her tales vary widely: they include historical tales, love stories, tragedies, comedies, poems, and burlesques. The stories depict genies, magicians, and legendary places, which are often intermingled with real people and geography, not always rationally; common protago-nists include the historical caliph (the chief Muslim civil and religious ruler), his vizier (chief of staff), and his court poet. Sometimes a character in Scheherazade's tale will begin telling other characters a story of his own, and that story may have another one told within it, resulting in a richly layered narrative texture. Different versions have different, individually detailed endings (in some Scheherazade asks for a pardon; in some the king sees their children and decides not to execute his wife; in still others, things happen that make the king distracted) but they all end with the king giving his wife a pardon and sparing her life. I particularly love this tale because it's not only a story itself, but also a story of stories, and the power of stories. *(Story details courtesy of Wikipedia.)*

There are a number of psychological reasons stories are so pow-erful. It's not simply that storytelling has been a primal form of communication or they help us get through difficult times, stories connect us to universal truths. Stories move beyond generational connections; they're maps of how we think. Think about this: if I tell you a fact, it's likely you might not remember it a week from now, but if I tell you a story that contextualizes that fact, then it's a whole other ballgame. Stories use both sides of the brain, triggering imagi-nation to allow listeners to become participants in the narrative. Stories also provide order and authenticate the human journey. In an article entitled "Our Stories, Ourselves," for the American Psycho-logical Association, Sadie F. Dingfielder quotes Amy Saidmain, head of SpeakeasyDC, a nonprofit theater group, who notes, "Storytelling isn't just how we construct our identities, stories *are* our identities."

If you want to engage your audience, remember that your job is to tell a story. Dr. Pamela Rutledge, director of the Media Psychology

Research Center, says this: "Stories are how we think. They are how we make meaning of life. Call them schemas, scripts, cognitive maps, mental models, metaphors, or narratives. Stories are how we explain how things work, how we make decisions, how we justify our decisions, how we persuade others, how we understand our place in the world, create our identities, and define and teach social values." Whether you are presenting your budget for next year or pitching to a new client, don't approach communication as if your job is merely to transmit a list of facts. A good story has a mission; it has a clear point of view. It has a beginning, middle, and end—they also have interesting characters, a plot, good dialogue, humor, and illustration.

As an art, storytelling is a blend of *ethos*, *logos*, and *pathos*. *Ethos* is the Greek word for "character;" from it the word "ethics" is derived. For our purposes, ethos is a speaker's character and credibility. It's inextricably linked to his or her philosophy, attitude, and code of conduct. *Logos* is Greek for "divine word," reason, the word of God. Logos is where we get our word "logic." Logic relies heavily on reason, examples, and fact. As a speaker, you must support your message clearly and convincingly by using accurate facts, examples, and details.

Finally, you need a dollop of *pathos*. Pathos is often stronger than logos. The word pathos comes from the Greek word for "suffering." From pathos comes the words "sympathy" and "empathy." While speakers should never prey on their audience's emotions, speakers must bear in mind that emotions are key components to the human psyche. We remember how someone makes us feel more than what they say. So when you craft your story or use one from current or ancient text, remember—you're looking to evoke emotion. Tell your story with an opening that grabs the listener's attention, then holds that attention with content, and finally closes with a lesson.

Storytelling depends on the storyteller. Is she or he the best person to tell the story? Is it their story? Is it secondhand? Storytelling depends on the words, devices, and tactics the storyteller decides to enlist. Are they genuine? Are they verifiable? How will an audience know whether or not what they've heard is true? Storytelling also relies on emotion. Has the storyteller used it to his or her advantage? What have they exaggerated? Have they been sneaky? Have they relied on hyperbole?

Benjamin Disraeli offers the advice, "Be amusing: never tell unkind stories: above all, never tell long ones." There's obviously a little more to it. Let's say you sit down and think, *Okay, let's see...this happened and then this happened—oh, and this happened right after.* Good stories aren't necessarily chronological. It's about "afflicting the comfortable and comforting the afflicted." It's about pointing out what you've noticed that no one else has—or, at the very least, taking the time to point out something that might not be obvious. Good storytelling begins with critical thinking. (Critical thinking—at least in the typical Western sense—clarifies goals, examines assumptions, discerns hidden values, evaluates evidence, accomplishes actions, and assesses conclusions.)

Critical thinking is what helps storytellers state their point of view. It's also the deciding factor as to whether or not the storyteller will get to her point, and it's what allows a storyteller to wade through general reasons and assumptions to offer sound reasons and takeaways as well as be able to foresee other possibilities and explanations. Furthermore, critical thinking is what helps the storyteller consider—whether through response or avoidance—overgeneralization, excessive skepticism, credibility problems, and the use of persuasive language. A critical thinker who is a good storyteller must be able to take a position. His story must remain relevant and to the point. The habits of a critical-thinking storyteller are this: we're curious—we ask questions; we're collaborative—we're willing to learn from others; we're creative—we like to find new ways to share ideas; we care—we're able to relate to others in a meaningful way; we communicate—we like to enlighten others as to what we believe and think and feel; and most importantly, perhaps above all else is that we're critical—we give reasons as to why we believe what we believe.

Three of my favorite questions are: Why? How? What if? Some of us come by critical thinking naturally (which means we were taught this as children), but if Nietzsche was right (I'm confident he was), critical thinking is like dancing—it's something we can learn. You can be sure that even if critical thinking was something you learned as a child, if you don't use it, you'll lose it. Just imagine a prima ballerina who takes a decade off from practicing her craft. To begin reigniting, sparking, and fueling the flames of your critical thinking skills, begin to interpret any number of topics at hand by asking questions like: What's happening? What does this mean? What's the best way to make sense of this? How can I help others make sense of this?

As you enlist your critical thinking arsenal in making decisions as to what, why, and how, keep in mind that the story you weave must be interesting. Storytellers need to first remove their emotional bias. In other words, just because you think you've got a humdinger of a tale doesn't mean everyone else will feel the same way. So how do you know what's interesting? I always ask myself three questions when it comes to the potential of a story: Is it a true story? Is it a good story? Is it a useful story? Then I ask three other people I trust whether they think the story is believable, whether they think the story is useful, and lastly, whether it is entertaining.

How do you craft a compelling, convincing vignette? Amy Said-man, whom I mentioned above as host and producer of the Speakeasy (an open mic storytelling for adults), emphasizes that there are two key elements to a good story: "Something has to happen...and it has to mean something." Ira Glass, creator and host of the weekly public radio anthology *This American Life*, noted that the sequences that held his attention all followed the same pattern: action—action—action—moment of reflection—repeat. Adding to these premises are three more clues. First, I want you to keep things simple: don't make your audience work too hard. Second, I want you to realize that just like how your presentation needs a rock star beginning and a rock star ending, so too does each story you tell within that presentation. Memorize the beginning and the end; improvise the middle. Third, mind the spine and cut the fringe; if you're story has six parts, each one of those parts must be essential—if there's a part of your story that's peripheral, so minor to be seen as nonessential, then make a cut to the narrative.

I really should not have to add this point, but you can never be too careful. While storytellers are often naturally prone to hyperbole, do not lie on stage to an audience in order to create a more interesting story. Don't lie about your military record or college degree. Don't lie about being present at a momentous occasion. Don't claim you were shot at when in fact they threw flowers. I understand that mistakes happen, but do your best to always tell the truth or give credit where credit is due. And remember, if a story has to be embellished to make it interesting or to fit your point, it's not the right story for the situation. Just as you shouldn't tell a joke that's not funny, you shouldn't tell a story that's not true. Never hem and haw. Speak your truth. This isn't easy in a world where everyone is waiting to be offended, but it's a part of being a rock star. Your listener will buy into what you have to say but you have to speak your truth.

What Speakers Can Learn from Screenwriters

Besides making magic with an empty slate and a blank screen, speakers can learn a lot of general tips from screenwriters. They have a lot in common. Screenwriters are also storytellers; they're sharers; they each distribute, broadcast, circulate, and transmit a message. Both speakers and screenwriters have a limited amount of time to get their point across; screenwriters are known to condense a lifetime in an hour and twenty minutes. Arguably, speakers must be even more efficient and agile than a screenwriter because they may have just five minutes or less to get to their punch line.

A good screenwriter is able to distill the message of the plot into a single sentence. Screenwriters understand their stories on a visceral level. Whether it's about choice or freedom, life or death, they know exactly what the genre is as well as its subgenre. There's also a screenwriter's sense of timing. Real time is not a lifetime—screenwriters use finesse to move quickly, "pan out" what needs to be perceived as expansive and do close-ups when the details are what make the difference.

Consider a screenwriter's sense of tidiness, collusion, and completeness. All too often, they must kill a few of their darlings. Ever hear of those actors who end up on the cutting room floor? Just because the scene was shot doesn't mean it will make it into the film. It's the same with crafting a speech. You might think you've got a fantastic anecdote, but if you don't have the material to transition it into your overall speech, cut it. If you've got one humdinger of an anecdote and one ancillary one (and it doesn't matter how much research it took to unearth it or how funny you can make the delivery), if it doesn't work within the overall framework of the entire presentation, you know what you need to do. It's absolutely essential you delete "scenes" that don't move/support your story/message along. Screenwriters do it all the time. Don't be afraid to give something a try, and don't be afraid to "film it" only to leave it on the cutting room floor. This is one of the reasons why you need to rehearse in order to tell a story well.

All of this leads to the idea that, as a speaker, you should have someone you trust to bounce ideas off. I run one of the largest political luncheon clubs in my state, and I begin every meeting with a monologue. I think I'm funny. And, frankly, on Sunday night when I am preparing, I'm hilarious, laugh-out-loud funny. Still, I always run all of my jokes by a dear friend who's on my board. I want to make absolutely certain I don't cross a line and offend anyone. Just because it's funny to me, doesn't mean it will be funny to others, and I cannot afford to fail. Another point to be made is that just because it's funny once won't mean it will be funny the second or third time around.

Another practice speakers can garner from screenwriters is storyboarding. Typically, the act of storyboarding involves the creation of a graphic organizer. Storyboards are images and illustrations displayed in a sequence in order to pre-visualize a film. First developed at the Walt Disney Studios in the early 1930s, storyboards are often an essential part of the creation process, especially for animation and action films.

Try this. Write the pitch—and this should include each separate anecdote, joke, fodder, fact, and/or detail—of your presentation on flashcards. While you're working on the distinct and separate components of your speech, consider and reconsider your theme/message. I don't do my best brainstorming in front of a computer; I still use pen and paper to sketch out my ideas. When crafting a message for a client or me, I use Post-it notes. I usually post three at the top for the main three ideas, and then I post down with three for each thought, and then three more until I see a pattern. Post-it notes are great because they can be moved easily and then can be put on a sheet of paper to be transferred to my computer for the final draft. The key is to use what I call "scatter-grams" so you don't lose any ideas that would make great asides or great answers for the questions that may come. A scatter-gram is a brainstorming device I enlist; I write down words or phrases that will prompt stories and associations. Then play around with the order to see what works. Seeing it all written out helps me figure out where my beginning ends, where my middle ends, and where my end begins.

This leads into still another thing we can learn from screenwriters: the simple and exquisite beauty of three acts. The three-act structure is exactly how you should approach the crafting of the beginning, middle, and end outline of your speech, lecture, or presentation. Aristotle's theory builds on this to state that because stories, typically Western ones, have a beginning, middle, and end, things happen—there's movement. That intelligent, sequential *movement* is what will grab and hold your audience's attention. On this topic, screenwriter, producer, and director Nora Ephron writes, "Structure is the key to narrative. These are the crucial questions any storyteller must answer: Where does it begin? Where does the beginning start to end and the middle begin? Where does the middle start to end and the end begin? In film school you learn these three questions as the classic three-act structure. This structure is practically a religion among filmmakers."

And so it should be with speechmakers. Americans are somehow conditioned to think in threes; besides Hollywood plots, the three-part story outline is common in folktales and Biblical tales. There's "Goldilocks and the Three Bears," "The Three Billy Goats Gruff," and "The Good Samaritan" with its three travelers. Or think boy meets girl, boy loses girl, boy gets girl in the end. Bob Dorough was right—for all of you who remember his *Schoolhouse Rock!* song, "Three Is a Magic Number."

Thinking in threes is good practice. It's also necessary when it comes to audience attention span. Remember that the average audience attention span is fifteen minutes and dropping? Gone are the days when speakers could hold an audience for hours on end. Unfortunately, your audience can't sit that long, nor do they want to. Most folks can't even watch a movie all the way through without getting up and getting popcorn or talking to their neighbor. Andrew Dlugan, editor and founder of *Six Minutes*, points out that when you use the three-part structure "your presentation gains warmth, familiarity, and understandability." For general speechwriting, he's found there're several three-part formats you can use:

- tell them what you're going to say—say it—tell them what you said,
- past—present—future
- introduction—body—conclusion,
- three stories
- three main points
- pros, cons, and recommendations.

No matter what you're trying to accomplish with your presentation, having the framework of a three-act structure puts you ahead of the curve. Screenwriters have known this since they began making movies. Storytellers have known it long before that. When you take advantage of what screenwriters can teach you, your speech is that much more captivating and balanced.

Persuasion, Emotions, and Information

In your career, you will give presentations that are meant either to persuade or to simply inform or educate. In each of these settings, you'll have two choices: you can be funny or you can be serious. Your decision depends, once again, on your audience and also on the topic you'll be giving. Sometimes a serious or tense topic can be lightened a little by a well-placed, tactful joke or bit of irony; sometimes it must be treated with total sobriety. And of course, some audiences respond better to the use of humor than others; it's your job to determine whether or not this is the case with your audience. Always keep in mind that the line between being funny and being offensive is very fine. If you're in doubt about the appropriateness of a joke, avoid it.

Find out if your audience is there to support you or to fight you. Will they question your position, or will they want to get on board with your program, campaign, or product? How can you figure this out? Ask the person who scheduled your presentation for information about your audience. If you don't plan for this in advance, your audience may ambush you.

If your goal is to persuade, there are a few pointers you need to be aware of. Because most folks have their minds made up based on emotional reasons rather than logical ones, persuasion might be one of hardest things you will ever do. If you want to change their minds, you'll need a pretty convincing argument.

There are basically two types of persuasion speeches that most coaches will teach. One uses an inspiring story to capture the audience's heartstrings and make them set aside their doubt about the situation just enough to swing their emotions over to the other side. You see this on TV commercials for everything from local animal shelters to children in other countries you can help for as little a thirty-two cents a day. Because your emotions are touched regarding the plight of others, you will give; you've been persuaded by inspiration. So consider your message for a moment. You may have to dig deep to find the human factor, the emotional string that ties your message to the hearts of your audience, but it's always there.

The other way to persuade is the simple ability to convince your audience through facts and data that can be used to support a particular position. Our bipartisan American political system is the perfect example of this. In fact, as I write, I am inundated by presidential pre-election chatter; both camps are backed by facts, stories, and real life situations of people being harmed by one party's policies or the other's. These are hard facts and can be verified (by both sides according to what they need) to convince voters at their core that people are being wronged unjustly and that they can do something about it by voting for this campaign. "A vote for us is a vote for right, truth and the American way..." Believe it or not, if they say it enough, some folks will regard it as truth and will be swayed to that side—at least until the next election.

You'd be wise to address the other side, those who do not agree with you at all. Once you know what you're up against in the listener's mind, you can break down those walls of dubiousness and be able to, in a sense, lay down tracks they can follow, whether they believe you or not. You'll undoubtedly come across the mentality of "I know what you say is true but I choose not to care or believe." For example, we all know that smoking is not good for your heath yet every day people smoke; they know it's bad for them but choose to ignore the facts for various reasons. Don't be frustrated by this mindset; it says more about your listener than your speaking abilities. Focus on making your presentation watertight and answering thoughtful, well-informed questions from audience members who actually want to hear your responses rather than voice their own opinions. I have always said that your ability to speak and persuade will always be backed up by your ability to answer the questions that will be forthcoming.

Speaking to inform or educate is easier because you can show facts and figures and give real-life examples of how a product/idea/mantra/whatever works, why the audience should use it, and how they will be better for doing so. When you speak to inform, you need strong, salient points of fact; you need to present them in a logical and mentally organized manner; you need to back up your information with credible sources to verify your points and be able to answer the questions that you know will come from those who are skeptical.

Find a unifying theme. In addition to imparting information, a speech must move people. The goal is to make the listeners think, care, respond, and act. This will help you organize the speech logically. Develop one or two good quotes, stories, and analogies, especially G-rated personal anecdotes. Insert them early in the speech and develop the central message from the opening.

Audiences Prefer Personal

It's imperative that as a rock star speaker you learn to craft and create your own unpredictable, personal stories. It's best if your audience hasn't heard what you have to say from other speakers. Most audiences have smidgen of what I call ADDD, Attention Deficit Disorder

Deliberately, which means that if they don't have to pay attention, they won't, so it is your responsibility to cajole them into listening.

If you can share good personal narratives with your audience, you will capture their hearts and minds. I have crafted many personal stories for use in my presentations so that I would have a connection with my audience on every level: as a business owner who has had great success and who has lost a business; as a politician who has won and lost; as a sibling who used to be a rambunctious kid and who is now a respected adult. I use these stories to show nuggets of who I am. As much energy as I have put into crafting my status as a rock star public speaker in order to instill confidence in my audience, sometimes it distances me from them. I use personal narratives to make a personal connection and share with my listeners where I came from and where I plan to go—something everyone can relate to.

One example I have of using personal stories (this is also a good example of creating collaborative distance) comes from my work with the Social Security Administration where I train Public Affairs Specialists. These days most everyone seems to be unhappy with SSA, so when I speak to them I say thank you. They're genuinely shocked, because they're rarely thanked for what they do. The reason I'm such a fan is that when I was a kid, my dad passed away. I can remember getting a large card stock check in the mail every month. These were my survivor benefit checks (a great gift the government gives kids to help with school books and other small expenses). When I say thank you to my PAS class, it totally disarms them until I ask, "Why did you stop them when I turned eighteen?" and they all break out with laughter.

During a break at a conference—this one was about public speaking—a lady came up to me with tears in her eyes to tell me that as a girl, she too had received those checks. She went on to say that she'd never in a million years have considered using her account as a personal storytelling anecdote about her life. And yet, that's all it takes. I can almost guarantee you'll find the fodder you need to craft rich stories from your own personal and professional life. Each of us has something in our past that has the power to help our audience identify with us. At the very least, our personal narratives can serve as general learning curves for others.

The trick is to make your script fit the situation. Have an understanding of the audience's needs and how you need to address them. Nothing is worse than a speaker who clearly gives the same talk to completely different audiences. This shows a total disregard for their intelligence and a lack of originality on the speaker's part.

I tell real stories from the stage, stories that are specific to the point that I want to make. For example, when I speak about how I learned to be great at sports, I mention that I am the youngest of five children, and I am the only girl. Growing up the youngest in my household, it was a matter of survival. At a young age, I learned how to punch hard and run fast. It has made a big difference in business and in politics.

In my family, there was never a distinction between my brothers' abilities and mine. I learned to be self-sufficient, forward thinking, and to have boundless energy because that's what they had. If I planned to live in that household, I too had to run on high speed. My brothers, as far as I could tell, never much thought to the fact that I was a girl. They taught me to play basketball, baseball, soccer, tennis, and volleyball, as well as horseback riding. I underwent this because, as my brother Joel told me a few years ago, "Deb, we never want you to be a boring date."

This story contains several elements my audience can relate to. First, it sets me up as someone who has come a long way from the only girl in a family of boys. I might have considered that a disadvantage, but instead I used it to help me excel not only in sports but in my career. This encourages the audience members to see themselves as people who can overcome their individual circumstances and even use them to their advantage. Second, it gives the audience a little personal information about me: even though I'm the celebrity, I'm also a real human being who grew up in a normal family. I got into fights with my brothers and made mistakes when I was learning. Finally, it adds an element of humor, especially in the last line. Being able to laugh a little at my expense puts the audience at ease with me.

A word of caution about personal stories: don't give out too much information. Have you ever been in line in a public place and someone is yakking on and on about their love life or recent surgery in detail? I cringe when I hear about business deals, checking accounts, and personal matters discussed in public. A little mystery is a good thing.

Writing "for the Ear"

If you've ever been to a Deb Sofield seminar, you've probably heard me say to write your speech *for the ear* and not for the eye. This means that as a speaker you need to find words your audience will easily hear and understand. This is an important guideline for speechwriting and public speaking. And though it may seem counterintuitive when you're writing, the ear is less interested in good grammar than it is in content and lyric.

Speaking succinctly and with clarity can make or break you as a speaker. Remember, words are symbols that you will use to express your ideas and feelings. Use words that are concrete, that are linked with things we see, hear, smell, taste, and touch. This will ensure that everyone is on the same page; they're all receiving the same message and there is little room for misinterpretation.

In today's environment, we are fraught with political correctness, and we are judged by the language we use. We've all heard the old adage about sticks and stones, but in this case words can not only inflict emotional pain but can also produce irrevocable damage to your career. We must always be aware of our audience members' sensitivities and chose our words wisely because some words have different meanings to different people, and similar words have different meanings: I can invite you to my house (structure) or my home (dwelling). I encourage you to remember the golden rule: *do unto others as you would have them do unto you.* This holds true for speaking. Poor word choices can wreak a career. So when you speak, choose words that are familiar and understandable to the listener and are easy on the ear. This is one of the fundamental rules for speechwriting and public speaking.

Part of creating a speech with natural flow and rhythm is being selective with the rules of grammar. Sound counterintuitive? Consider this: talking is different from writing, and sometimes, correct grammar and complete sentences sound unnatural. Certainly talking without contractions (don't, won't) is unnatural and will make you sound stiff. However, this doesn't mean that you can ignore grammar altogether. Many grammatical mistakes will make you sound uneducated and unprofessional, rather than casual. For example, you should always know how to correctly pronounce all of the words in your speech. I work as an interview coach in the pageant business. At a local pageant the interviewer questioned one of the girls about "youth in Asia,", while intending to say "euthanasia." The interviewer's Southern drawl nearly cost a young woman her crown.

If ever you're in doubt, remember that correct grammar is not offensive to anyone, while incorrect grammar can be offensive to everyone who knows better. Read and learn. Listen and learn. Embrace the local vernacular only up to the point your audience is entertained by or accepting of it. Be careful, but remember that some grammar rules apply more to the written word than to the spoken word.

One of the best ways to make your speech sound natural is to avoid extraneous words. The ancient Greeks were right when they said that speech is the mirror of the soul. When you speak, it's your soul that's bared, your personal and professional image reflected in every word. In ancient Rome, sculptors sometimes sought to conceal surface cracks in a statue with the aid of melted beeswax. A buyer, deceived into believing that she was purchasing a flawless piece of marble, placed such a statue proudly in her atrium. A few weeks later the beeswax dried out, crumbled away, and left the original cracks exposed. This trickery became so prevalent that reputable sculptors began to guarantee their works as *sine cera*, "without wax." You are not in the business of carving statues out of marble, but you do something similar. You carve communication out of words.

Avoid slang or idiomatic expressions. We've already covered "I'm sorry" and "Let me ask you a question," but there are plenty of other "crutch phrases" you should avoid. One in particular is the "honestly" phrase. When you say things like "to be honest" or "to tell the truth," it makes the rest of what you're saying sound insincere. When I hear "honestly," I think, *Well, that's probably a first. Aren't you honest all the time?* Don't give away your power by using these trite phrases. Other trite phrases to avoid include the following:

- as you can see
- if you will
- it is indeed an honor and a privilege
- I'd like to take a few minutes
- each and every one (grammarians cringe with this one: choose one or the other)
- what I am trying to say
- in closing/in conclusion
- as I have said before
- and so forth and so on
- et cetera, et cetera

These expressions are fillers (wax), and they don't cover up the flaws in your speech transitions. Repetition can have the same effect. If you are emphasizing an important point, repetition is okay, but a continual use of the same word or phrase over and over can be distracting.

And then there's something I call supercalifragilisticexpialidocious superlatives: "If you say it loud enough, it's really quite atrocious." Be subtle in your speech. Let your ideas make their point by the careful words that you choose and be wary of superlatives. Statements such as: "This is absolutely and positively essential," and "This is true beyond any possible shadow of a doubt," come off as insincere and over-tried—and they often undermine themselves.

A good sense of humor can save you in a speech. But you must be careful that your humor is above board and funny to all of your listeners. A good line or funny saying can level the playing field and can cut through hard feelings and set you up for success.

No matter what you do, do not swear from the platform. Vulgarity is rarely appropriate in public speaking. Yes, I know a few national speakers who do swear, but most of us in the business aren't impressed by it. You can always think of a better word than a swear word. People may begin to question your intelligence if you rely on the vulgar word choice. Educated, professional people should not speak this way. Think about the words that you use and what your audience hears when you use them. Remember, it is not just what you say but what listeners hear that matters.

And by the way—if you *do* say, "in conclusion," please conclude. I once heard a speaker who said "in closing" six times.

Closing Power

Once you've nailed your opening, secured your content, and worded it for maximum power and effect, you'll want to find a way to finish memorably. Just as you must have a great opening, you must close powerfully. It's psychologically proven that people remember best what they hear first and last. Sometimes the middle part gets lost in our memory, so your closing needs to be as powerful as your opening. You want your audience to leave the room pondering what you just said.

So how do you craft an ending that works? If you've remembered what I've taught—to begin with the end in mind—everything you've crafted in your presentation needs to have had a point of purpose; now is the time to tie up the loose ends with your closing statement. I have a few closers I like to use: sometimes, like a final countdown, I reiterate the main points of my speech; sometimes I use a quote or saying that serves as a final thought; sometimes I thank the audience for having me (if I have not done this at the beginning of my talk, saving it to the end seems to pack a better punch); sometimes I close with a shocking statistic (it's tricky to add new information at closing time, but if it's a major and startling fact of what could happen if the advice/content of the speech is not heeded, then such a statement will likely prompt conversation, and even better, action); and sometimes I end with my standard line, "I'm Deb Sofield, and I approve this message." I know that phrase is from the world of politics but it seems to work for me. Find what works for you and craft it for your success.

When you consider that your audience will remember your first and last words. Make sure your last words stay with them long after they leave the building. Like oatmeal on a cold winter morning, you want your message to stick to the ribs, so as they wander home, they can mull over your speech and digest the meaning. So prepare ahead of time and have those though-provoking, memorable first and last words ready, and I can't say this enough: *your opening and ending should be memorized*. I want you to have the value of eye contact with your waiting audience. Never read your closing line. Look up and see your audience. Then give your final word.

If your ultimate goal is to deliver meaningful content, as it probably is, remember that you cannot achieve this goal until you have figured out how to tweak your appearance and use your voice in a consistent manner. Using the triple-threat delivery we've discussed in Section II—the look, the voice, and the content—you can now let go of the fear and focus on how to be the best rock star presenter that I know you can be.

Section III:

ROCK STAR

The first five chapters have covered a lot of ground when it comes to creating rock star presentation skills. I've provided techniques that will enable you to put the whole package together, to create a powerful presence before your audience, and to become what I call a triple threat—someone who can look the part, act the part, and sound the part of a world-class, rock star speaker.

No lecture attendee has ever said, "I hope the speaker is boring. I hope they waste my time. I hope I get nothing out of the next hour of my life." Okay, there may be the occasional audience member who genuinely wants to take a nap. To that I say, give them a reason to pay attention. Give them a reason to open their eyes and take notice.

Remember to show your audience that you love what you're doing and that feeling good is easy. Do this by being enthusiastic and animated. Remember to engage your audience; find a way to relate to them with a personal anecdote or an appeal to their generational culture that

I defined in Chapter Five. The Rule of Connectivity states that the more the audience can connect with you on some level or another, the more they will like you, listen to what you are saying, and believe in your vision.

Don't forget to pay attention to those who have gone before you, you can learn from their triumphs and their failures; you can use their stories as a compass and steer yourself, and your career, down the path you choose. You can learn to master their techniques in order to create a message that moves your audience, either to laughter or tears or both, but no matter how brightly your star burns, you'll need to continually work on your delivery.

Whether it's to adjust to an ever-changing audience or to ensure that your message continues to be relevant, interesting, and evocative, communicating with people takes work, but once you've had your first couple of speeches, you'll be more confident. You'll know your story, be secure in your facts, and recognize where your delivery shines—and where it could use a slight polishing. You'll start to see that you can do this without fear, because when the lights come up and the audience leaves and you're still standing, honing your message for another stellar performance, you'll start to see that there is absolutely nothing to be afraid of!

6

BEFORE THE GIG

Talent is cheaper than table salt. What separates the talented individual from the successful one is a lot of hard work.

—STEPHEN KING

If there's one thing that I've learned in the past twenty years, it's that people *want to be inspired*. The demands of everyday life can be exhausting—people are hungry for inspiration, encouragement, and camaraderie. They want to hear your vision in the hopes it will move them—to change their future actions, renew how they view the world, or in some other meaningful way. This is something I tell every speaking client, and it's something that's essential to remember as a speaker.

Most audience members want to be engaged and enticed. They want to participate, learn, and contribute. People want to know that they matter, that they too can make a difference—and they want to know more about others who are affecting change, paying it forward, and doing things in their own distinct way. I love to teach, to speak, and to mentor about public speaking. I can do it every day of my life because I can see how it can change another person's life. In just a few hours, I can make a difference, and that motivates me. Ultimately, by sharing our vision, we share the best part of who we are.

Whether you're offering the annual fiscal report to your shareholders or clarifying how one can use Pinterest as a marketing tool in small business, remember that most anytime you speak before a large audience, it's because *they invited you there.* They want to hear what you have to say, and everyone is pulling for you. No one wants you to fail. Why? Because before you even arrived at the venue, someone had the foresight and the confidence in you to invite you to speak. They would not invite you if they didn't believe that you have something important to offer. Your audience also wants you to succeed and do well, so accept this as something that's working for you. This is one of the greatest gifts you can receive as a speaker, so bask in your audience's preemptive goodwill, and you will do well.

That said, I want to reiterate that as a speaker you should know as much as you can about the people who "want you to speak." Be sure to know why your audience has come to hear you. Is it an obligation, required by work? Is it a free chicken dinner? Is there a reward? What do they expect to learn? What is their attitude toward the subject or their position on the issue? To be an effective speaker, you must first know your audience—or at least have a vague idea of why they're coming to see you speak—and then read your audience.

I once spoke in my home state to a political women's dinner club. I come from the state that ranks fiftieth in the nation for the number of women in public office, and I planned a great speech called "Throw the Bums Out." It was a funny, smart-aleck speech about the state legislature. But I did not do my homework. I did not research my audience. While I was walking around beforehand, introducing myself to many of the women, they were all introducing me to their husbands—the exact elected officials my speech mocked. I couldn't rewrite my presentation fast enough to weed out all the funny comments directed at the female-only audience, so I limped along, got through with a mediocre speech, and got out of there. They have never invited me back. This was completely my error and a hard lesson learned.

The takeaway here is that you must know to whom you're speaking. Do your homework. This experience has made me better prepared to share my successful speech-making techniques with you. I have experienced the pitfalls firsthand, and I will do everything I can to avoid letting that happen again, to me and to you.

Speaker Notes

Even though I speak from notes, I write my speeches out verbatim for practice and review, and I have my clients do the same because I believe the discipline of writing out your speech is important. The process of either writing or typing out your speech helps you get to know your topic better, which makes you more comfortable when you are speaking; and the better you know your topic, the less you need to rely on your notes. I don't recommend reading your speech verbatim, as this can come across sounding stilted and stiff. However, even though I don't read my speech, I do keep it handy so I don't miss an important point (and can easily get back on track if an audience member interrupts me with a question or comment). I recommend that you do the same.

Once you have written out your entire speech, creating crib notes, or a concise set of notes summarizing your main points, also helps you become familiar with your topic and how each point leads to the next. Crib notes should create triggers that remind you of the next point in your speech. Good notes will mean the difference between awkward stumbling and smooth delivery, especially when you first give a new speech. Therefore, I've put together several points to keep in mind for writing effective crib notes.

As a speaker, I have always used what I consider the speaker's page format for your success. For the border of my page, I use half an inch from the top, one inch on each side, and two inches from the bottom of the page. This helps prevent me from having to drop my head to see the information at the bottom of the page; I can see everything just by dropping my eyes. This creates a much smoother and more professional delivery, and it's much easier to keep your place on the page.

Be sure to use a font and font size that are easy for you to read. Since I don't wear my glasses on stage, I use twenty-point Times New Roman font to keep my pages easy to see. And I encourage you to number your pages on the top and on the bottom. If you use a large font, you won't necessarily have to double-space.

Keep your notes in a folder that you can open easily, rather than a notebook that you click to open. In a silent room full of a lot of people, this can sound like the kiss of death, and it may set off your nerves. You don't want the audience to count your papers, so don't flip them. Instead, slide your papers from left to right so that when you're done speaking all the pages are in a backward order.

Remember, even though you've written or typed a copy of your opening and closing lines, memorizing them will allow you to deliver your opener and closer without the distraction of checking your notes. This way you can maintain eye contact and hold on to that personal connection while you articulate those two crucial components of your presentation. It's ok to have them in your crib notes and with you during your speech, but having them memorized will give you a great boost of confidence because you'll step on the stage knowing you're going to blow them away and leave them with a bang.

A Note on PowerPoint

Speaking on complex topics can be tricky, but you probably already know that. In cases like this, imagery can help. Even though I've never been a fan of PowerPoint (and I get a lot of grief for it), I fully understand that sometimes, due to the complexity of an issue, you might need to use a slide or two. However, you have to be careful about using PowerPoint and other multimedia crutches. Be prepared for technology to fail. This happens, and if you're not prepared, then you will be trying to recover from the beginning. Death by PowerPoint is slow and painful for all of those involved.

I don't cling to PowerPoint because *I am the show*, not my slides. It's the same for you. Your audience has come because they want to hear *you*. They want to see *your* face as you describe the situation. They want to feel the connection, not stare at a white screen with too many words and unnecessary graphics. The main reason I despise PowerPoint is because it's so often used incorrectly. Maybe you learned that visual aids are one way to distract your audience from you, the speaker. Maybe you used this device as a means of controlling your own fear factor. If you've been following along and preparing yourself in the visual, vocal, and verbal, you will not need a reason to hide behind a visual aid.

That said—there is a time and place for PowerPoint. You know when that time is necessary, and you will have to balance your time when you craft your presentation to include the PowerPoint aspect.

It should not be your entire presentation. Make sure that what appears on your slides is relevant and *absolutely* necessary.

Now, if you must use slides, there are a few things to keep in mind. First, keep the lights on bright; do not turn down the lights to show your slides. Why? For the simple reason that most of us are tired, and if you turn off the lights, folks will take a nap. Also, the lights need to be on bright because slides should simply reinforce what you say (not word for word), and the audience should be able to see your face as you speak. Second, use no more than six words on a slide, and keep your slide count (for an hour presentation) between ten and twelve. Third, make a point to buy *cool, engaging* stock photography—don't use the typical images everyone else is using, and if appropriate, find a signature ending slide.

Guy Kawasaki, CEO of Garage Technology Ventures, a venture capital fund focusing on startups with novel technologies, has probably listened to a lot of speakers, presentations, and proposals in his career. He's famous for his 10-20-30 Rule for PowerPoint:

- **10 slides** are the optimal number to use for a presentation.
- **20 minutes** is the longest amount of time you should speak.
- **30-point font** is the smallest font size you should use on your slides.

He also states that "[t]he more media a speaker uses, the less he or she has to say." This is coming from the CEO of a firm specializing in novel technology! So, *when in doubt, do without.* Again, remember that your audience came to hear you speak, not read your slides. They could have done that from the comfort of their own office, living room, or son's baseball game.

If someone asks you to create a PowerPoint slideshow, or you are considering it to enhance an aspect of your own presentation, try following these basic rules. I picked them up a long time ago, so I am unsure of whom to credit for their authorship.

- Coordinate what you say with what the audience is seeing. There is nothing more annoying than for a speaker to be off on their slides so the conversation and slide do not match.

- Remove or delete the visual when it is finished. I like to take my screen to black so the audience will focus back on me and not doze off or mentally argue with my slide even though I have moved on to another point in my presentation.

- Position your body to face the audience when you speak. Do not speak to the screen behind you. I see this all the time and it makes me crazy. Audiences can read the slide. Don't read it aloud to them. Remember, PowerPoint just enhances what you're saying; it is not the show.

- Again, keep the lights on bright. I know your audience is going to say, "Turn the lights down so we can see." Don't do it. What they really mean is: "Turn the lights down so we can *sleep*." Keep the lights on bright so they can see your facial expressions and stay awake.

- Use a title on every slide. This is a standard rule. Follow it to keep your audience in line with your presentation. It's also a good idea to brand your slides with your contact information or your website.

- Include only one thought or image per slide. Since most places, companies, and TEDtalks force you to keep to a few slides, people often compensate by cramming more than one big idea per slide. This is not a good idea because if you can't tell it, then you can't sell it.

- Practice using the PowerPoint program and pointer. I shouldn't have to state this, but for the record, I will remind you that creating your PowerPoint at midnight to give the next day is not a great idea. You really need to practice before you give your stellar PowerPoint so that you are familiar with what comes next.

When you use PowerPoint, make your slides available to your audience in a Dropbox file after your presentation. This will also help prevent your audience from feverishly trying to copy everything down in lieu of listening to what you're saying. Conversely, have your PowerPoint ready in a handout version in case the system goes down. You cannot cancel your presentation and blame the technology. You must stand and deliver. Remember, you can't dress up boring content with a PowerPoint presentation; audiences will know if you're cheating them on substance with smoke and mirrors.

Scheduling Gigs and Travel

The time of day you speak will affect your presentation so determine when you do best as a speaker. Are you a morning person? A night person? Are you high energy or more laid back? Morning and afternoon speakers need to be loud and alive; after-dinner speakers need to slow it down and tell stories that are lighthearted since most in the audience have likely had a long day. Usually I tend to do well in the morning and after lunch since I have high energy. Sometimes I am asked to charge up an audience in the evening, but that's rare. It's a lot like being on a radio show. In the morning, for drive time, you need to be woken up; you want a show that is witty, funny, and depending on the station, a little bawdy. Midmorning shows are slower, informative but with an edge. By midafternoon, some stations will have real-life, personal, and news shows. At evening drive time, around five o'clock, we're back to loud and funny. After dinner are your more thoughtful news, personal interest, and motivational shows. So know what time of day works for you and do your best to schedule accordingly.

Breathe

The most common reason for fear before speaking is feeling unprepared. I always tell clients that this is also the easiest source of fear to overcome. All you have to do is practice, practice, and practice. So lock yourself in a bathroom with a mirror and rehearse, or use a video camera to record yourself practicing. This will allow you to see what the audience will see and catch any awkward movements before you get on the stage. I also encourage people to talk out their speech. Don't practice in silence. You need to speak it out until you get the "feel" of it. Remember the speaker's code: the ear can fix what the eye can't see, so practicing out loud is paramount.

There are some other wonderfully simple ways to relax. Isometrics can break the feeling of fear. You can either squeeze your hands together tightly for fifteen seconds then let go in successions of threes or simply press your fingertips together, one thumb and one finger at a time. Either physical practice disrupts the circuit of fear that your brain is transmitting. It's tricking your brain into focusing on something besides jitters and anxiety. A great thing about these isometrics is that your audience won't notice you doing them.

Face "freezing" is also handy, though you'll want to do this without an audience. Do a face freeze: scrunch up your face, freeze, and hold for fifteen seconds, then release. Another thing I want you to do is open your mouth as wide as you can and hold it until your jaw naturally loosens; ultimately, this helps with your pace—you need your mouth to be limber, so stretch it. Some folks find this activity calming, as it releases nervous energy. Another trick, as simple as it sounds, is to take a few deep breaths. Fill your lungs with air, hold, and release. This will increase blood flow and in turn can reduce mental and physical fatigue as well as stress.

Drink plenty of water! I can't say this enough. Water will lubricate you vocal chords, energize your muscles, and stay off dehydration jitters. Your brain needs oxygen to function and drinking water ensures that it gets all the oxygen it needs. Drinking plenty of water also ensures that your electrolyte levels remain high enough to allow your nerves to communicate with your brain quickly and efficiently. So keep your cognitive performance high and your stress levels low by making sure you're hydrated.

Again, before beginning a speech, check the following: isometrics, face freeze, pace, breath, and water. Try an isometric exercise: clasp your hands together tightly and hold for fifteen seconds and release, then repeat. Set your pace: take a minute, walk, and breathe; walk and breathe. Go to the restroom, wash your hands, breathe deeply, take a deep breath, hold it, and release.

Lights, Camera ... You're On

Survey the venue well before you're on. Does the backdrop clash with your clothes? (While I'm on the campaign trail, I kept two jackets in the car in case my red dress clashed with the crushed orange velvet state curtain; you never want to distract your audience.) Is there a cord on the floor? Are you walking up steps without a handrail? You want to give yourself enough time to go home and change if necessary, so if you can check out the venue the day before you speak, that's ideal. You may not always get that option, but if you can, take advantage of it.

On the day of your speech, arrive early—even a few minutes makes a difference—to make sure things work. If you speak often enough, you'll begin to have a routine. My preparatory ritual before I stand and deliver is to pray over the room. There's something about the quiet before the crowd arrives that calms and centers me. This habit demands nothing more than for me to stand as close to the middle of the space that I can and say a quick prayer to recognize and affirm that I'm just the messenger and I need all the help I can get as a speaker whose words have the power to touch hearts and change lives.

Whether or not you take the time to bless your space, I can't say it enough: Check your equipment. Check your equipment. Check your equipment. Make it a priority to test the sound system before speaking, and if that's not possible, ask the host to do this for you. Ask the sound person to join you in the room and do a microphone check. Nothing is more annoying than a speaker who cannot be heard or who is reverberating off the walls. To avoid creating a sound barrier between you and the audience, the microphone should be level with your mouth, about six inches away. Make sure to be familiar with how to adjust the microphone in case someone changes the height or if you are speaking after someone who's taller or shorter than you. Never blow into a microphone. Simply talk normally and let the sound system do the broadcasting.

You'll also need to consider the arrangement of the chairs to the sound system and lighting. The overall climate of the room can make a big difference in the way a presentation is received. Seating is critical to a successful presentation. You must consider not only interaction but also safety and comfort as well. Semicircular and straight theater styles enjoy one advantage: the audience is sitting very close together. When audience members are seated on a curve, they can look to their left and right and see the faces of each person in the row. This seating style helps an audience join in the conversation. This setup also allows the audience members to see the speaker without having to turn their head sharply. This togetherness allows laughter to pass immediately from one person to another. Laughter is contagious. Many people will laugh just because they see others laughing.

You want to make sure people sit as close as possible to the front of the room. This may mean removing chairs or roping off seats at the back of the room. Your host should know roughly how many people to expect, and you can adjust seating accordingly. If possible, seat for the least amount of distraction; no one should have to crawl over more than six people to get out of the row.

Always try to stand as close as you can to the first row; this closeness will add familiarity to the audience. If you're in a place where the seating is fixed, don't despair. If the seats can't move, you can. Be more animated and move around. This will cause the audience to move their heads to see you and connect with others around them. Your effectiveness as a speaker is only realized when the audience can actually see you. They want to see your face, your expressions, and your body language. It is easier to establish a bond when the speaker and audience can see each other. Create an atmosphere conducive to laughter and interaction. And so we're clear, when I say move, I mean roughly within a three-foot radius. The thing you don't want to do is move around so much that your audience can't keep up with you. Recently I was a speaker at a major event; the keynote was a guy that basically did everything wrong (shame on him). He stood at the front of the room where he posed a few questions to the audience (none of which were compelling or even interesting). He then proceeded to walk around the entire room, up and down aisles. The poor videographer couldn't keep track of him. Even worse, it made it difficult for the audience to focus on his message.

Don't become a barrier to your own message. We want to minimize all distractions that are within our control. So when you're on stage and you've made sure—beforehand—that there's water available (preferably room temperature), it's okay for you to take a drink of water while you're speaking, but what's not okay is for you to say, "Hold it, let me take a drink..." Just take your sip and move on. Also, whatever you do, don't drink anything with milk before you speak—milk causes phlegm, and it's hard to clear your throat with milk coating it. Likewise, be careful about too much sugar, skip the soft drinks, and do not drink anything cold, as it will chill your vocal chords. Do not drink wine or other alcoholic beverages before you speak. (I had a client who said to me, "Deb, I'm so much better after a glass of wine," to which I replied, "You only think you are.") Water, unsweetened tea, or black coffee is all I recommend.

Another little-known tip is to not brush your teeth before a speech because that mint or cinnamon toothpaste will dry you out, and you'll have a hard time speaking. Brush in the morning and save your mint for when you're done speaking. (It's nice to have fresh breath when everyone rushes the stage to shake your hand!)

Introducing Rock Stars, Even Humble Ones

Your credentials set the stage, so your introduction is key. It gives you the chance to build yourself up in such a way as to pique the audience's interest. It should tell your audience just enough to make them want to know more or be interested enough to stop and listen to what you have to say. Your introduction should get them to put down their salad forks to hear about the person who is just about to take the lectern.

Openings and introduction styles are subjective, so you need to find what works best for you and follow the proper protocol. However, nobody wants to hear a list of your degrees. What folks want is a connection to you, a detail that draws them to you. I would much prefer that the person introducing me say that I recently won a big award, I just got back from speaking in Russia, and my book is a *New York Times* best seller.

Do not let the person introducing you ramble on or make up silly stuff. I have heard the most awful introductions that made me cringe for the speaker. Another awful way to introduce a speech is when your moderator says, "Well, our speaker today is Deb Sofield. You all know Deb, so I don't have to say anything more about her." First of all, it's very unlikely that everyone in your audience knows you. Secondly, this doesn't create any connection between you and your audience. And, thirdly, it didn't set me up for success, and that will kill the spirit before the event begins.

Your moderator has a job to do, and you need to hold him or her to it. Moderators can set the stage for you, for your accomplishments, and for your vision. To that point, you need to write out your introduction and send it in advance or take it with you for the person who will be introducing you. Even if I've already sent my introduction, I keep two copies in my briefcase in case the moderator forgot or lost the copy I provided. I've never had someone say, "No thanks, I think I'll just wing it." They were thrilled to have something concrete and written down. And the best part is that when the introduction is amazing, you *and* your moderator are successful in the audience's eyes.

Your best bet is to have a minimum of two introductions: a funny one and a standard one. Depending on your audience, you can choose what will pique their interest in you the most. *Do* tell your audience your credentials so they'll be proud to know you, but don't transmit a list of facts. Give them something to remember you by. Many times, I encourage my clients to sum up their reputation in one word and then use it in their introduction. Do yourself a favor and label yourself. If you use it, others will pick it up and refer to you in your new title. It can be Auctioneer, Marketing Maven, Sales Superman, Benevolent Dictator, whatever fits—polish it up and use it.

I labeled myself when I was campaigning. I used to joke that I was the Hammer. If it landed on my desk at city hall, it would get done in a timely manner, and believe it or not, that moniker stayed with me all eight years on council and still to this day. Some folks still refer to me as the Hammer or Bosslady.

Here are two standard introductions for you to follow when writing an introduction for yourself. A personal introduction should include the following:

- your name and title
- an explanation of what you do
- interesting facts such as awards or accomplishments

If something is extraordinary, let it stand on its own.

A professional introduction should include the following:

- your name and title
- your education and coursework
- recognized community service, boards, and commissions

Whatever you do, do not send your resume. Instead, send a personal profile statement about yourself; it will better set you up for success.

As the moderator makes my introduction, many times, I will start to walk to the stage with a big smile and maybe a wave, but certainly an energetic walk and enthusiastic presence that will fill the room. After a brief thank-you to whomever is hosting you, tell folks who you are, but only if it's not obvious. Do not give them your entire biography or resume but give just a bit more about what is to come from the person in front of them. Many times I will weave in that I'm the youngest of five siblings, and the only girl. I do this to prep the audience for my punch line that there is nothing that they can do to offend me since I've survived all my brothers and their friends.

Preparation Trumps Fear

When it comes to fighting fear, there's a lot to be said for preparedness. Once you get your before-the-gig process streamlined, the whole act of speaking will become easier. You'll have less fear because you'll have less to be fearful about: you've already perfected your look, your voice, and your content, and now you can check off the items above one by one so that by the time you're standing up to speak, everything will be set. You won't have to worry about forgetting anything. You'll already have a great speech that you're passionate about and familiar with, and that you've crafted especially for your audience; you'll be wearing comfortable clothes that make you look and feel great; and you'll have a stellar introduction already written that will make the audience sit up and pay attention before you've even begun to speak.

Fear comes from the unknown. That's why we are slowly breaking down the process of speaking into all its facets, so you can become familiar, and then comfortable, and then confident with each one. It's all about making the process natural, second nature. When you are a natural speaker, there is nothing to fear.

7

THE PERFORMANCE

Act as if what you do makes a difference. It does.
—WILLIAM JAMES

Do you remember the first concert you attended? Most people do. But do you remember every concert you've ever attended? Probably not. Do you remember some of them? Hopefully—and if you do, they are probably the ones that stirred your emotions and energized you, the ones that made you feel something. This is what your speech should be like—an unforgettable concert. Remember, you are a rock star! In this chapter, you're going to learn how to make your speech one of the memorable ones.

If you're new to speaking, this might mean you need to fake it until you make it, and that's okay. Contrary to the title of my book, it's okay to speak with a bit of fear, especially at first. Fear is a great motivator, and really, most everyone speaks with a little bit of fear—or at least they should at first. Overcoming fear is incredibly empowering, and believe it or not, it can make you into a better speaker.

Energy and Electricity

Dear reader, you can use all of what I suggest in this book, but without this ingredient, you'll fail to be your very best. Energy is synonymous with life. You must have energy—it's the lifeblood of a presentation. It makes you seem interesting, passionate, easier to understand, natural, professional, and confident. Without this energy, your audience will fill the void with restlessness, and you will lose them. Your speaking energy will keep and capture an audience and make them glad they came since they're now charged up on your energy. No one wants to hear a dead speaker—you need to be a rock star, and you accomplish that with your energy. Whether it's from nerves or excitement, energy is what sustains you when you feel the weight of the event on your shoulders.

When you step out in front of the audience, remind yourself that this is the moment you've been waiting for. All the preparation you've put into looking and sounding your best is about to pay off. You'd be inhuman if you didn't have some nervous energy. Remember—nervous energy can easily be transformed into engaging passion! So as you're speaking, do not forget your vision. Do not forget your energy and vitality. Do not forget your posture. In essence, don't forget your look, your voice, or your content. If your audience's response is neutral, then wake them up with a startling fact or figure. If the attitude is favorable, make sure you are lively, true, and engaging.

A great way to show your enthusiasm is to move around the platform. Step forward to emphasize a point. Step backward to withdraw and bring the audience toward you. If you've stepped forward too many times, during a pause or transition take a few steps back. Always use the whole body as opposed to just using a few hand gestures or bending from the waist and not moving the whole body; it's easier on the eyes.

As you move, be sure that you are using controlled emotion. If your only goal was to convey information, you could have just handed out a report. A speech has some emotion. A good speech might have humor, anger, commitment, and learning. Sometimes as a presenter, you might need to show a little bit of righteous indignation. There are some things that make you angry. You can show flashes of frustration, anger, or exhaustion, but be careful: too much, and they might think you're a flake. Absolutely no jumping on the couch like Tom Cruise did on *Oprah*, or screaming like Howard Dean after he placed third in Iowa when he appeared to be rocketing to presidency. (This is affectionately known as the "I Have a Scream Speech.") Keep a lid on the crazy.

I have heard many a good speaker become great when they fell in love with their topic, because it shows. This is one way to apply the Rule of Connectivity I discussed earlier in Chapter Three, and it is one feature for which an enthusiastic speaker strives. That's energy. Have you ever sat in on a lecture or a speech of some kind and walked away with a warm fuzzy feeling inside? It's like a pat on the back, a friendly hug, or an A on a college paper. It says that you understood, that you got it, that you are an intelligent being. Isn't that the kind of feel-good message you would like to give your audience?

The Ceiling Is Falling

When it comes to being a speaker, there's an unspoken yet innate responsibility to care for your audience. No, I don't mean that you have to like them or feed or water them or even ever have to see them again, but while you have the microphone, *you are responsible* for their care. When you stand before any audience, you become the captain of the ship, the shepherd of the flock. This means having a handle on the audience's interest and comfort levels as well as bigger issues that may or may not come up. Let's start small and work our way up to crisis.

A speech is a public discussion and not a legal document. Don't speak at or down to your audience, but speak with them. And remember that an audience's attention span is about fifteen minutes and getting shorter all the time. If at all possible, keep your speech short, and know that the listener's attention span is short. You can even acknowledge this fact and make a joke out of it to help keep your listeners interested and to reassure them that you aren't going to ramble on.

As the presenter, you can tell if your audience is cold, hot, uncomfortable, or antsy. Read and respond to their needs. That shows respect for them, and they will appreciate it. I have never had an audience complain that they got too many breaks to go the bathroom or stretch their legs. By talking about the audience and caring for them, you will win them over.

Sometimes caring for the audience means managing unpredictable incidents. Once when I was speaking at a conference in Florida, there was a terrible storm. The room where I was speaking had drop ceiling tiles. In a loud burst, one of the tiles fell right next to me. Sensing we had a problem, I had the group get up and move to another room until the storm had passed. I knew that if we didn't relocate, the audience would be distracted, wondering when and where another tile would fall. Ultimately, I was in control; these people had entrusted me with their time and attention, and so I had to make the call that would enable them to get the most out of my presentation.

As a speaker you have a responsibility to take care of the people before you. You must be willing to do whatever it takes to keep the audience comfortable. As I outlined in Chapter Three, your facial expression is a big part of your body language. When the microphone goes dead or the lights go off, keep your chin up and level. Your actions and reactions will be remembered long after the lights come on.

Negative Banter and Other Difficulties

Despite the most arduous preparations, it's not always possible to prevent unfortunate situations. Learning to respond with grace enables you to keep things moving and salvage just about any situation.

Negative banter is one of my worst-case scenarios. I equate negative banter to what occurs in a high school class where the teacher has lost touch with his or her students. This can happen for any number of reasons. Possibly the teacher doesn't love teaching and is only going through the motions, or has become disengaged from the students and does not appeal to their interests. It could also be an us-against-you mentality in the class. What ensues is that the students are no longer listening to the teacher; they are having their own private conversations, or they are responding negatively directly to the teacher. Most of us witnessed or even participated in a classroom scenario like this during our scholastic careers, and as speakers, even the best of us will be forced to navigate such a situation at some point.

I would like to believe that this does not happen among adults in a business context. But in reality, it does happen from time to time—and for very similar reasons. Remember to show your audience that you *love* what you are doing. Do this by being enthusiastic and animated. Remember to engage your audience; find a way to relate to them with a personal anecdote or an appeal to their generational culture that I defined in Chapter Five. The Rule of Connectivity states that the more the audience can connect with you on some level or another, the more they will like you, listen to what you are saying, and believe in your vision. You can try talking positively about and to the audience during your performance. One of the marks of an effective speaker is that you can talk less about yourself and more about those who have come to hear you speak. If you can say the names of people in your audience that's good, or at least it keeps them awake. Commend them for something good they have done. It will go a long way.

You want to avoid an us-against-you mentality, too. If this develops, don't panic but *listen*. Listen to what gave you that impression and respond directly to it. In most situations, this is a misunderstanding or a miscommunication and you can overcome it. Sometimes you can restate an issue so all can find agreement—or consensus, or at the very least clarity. If it's a topic that's polarizing, then you might also choose to make a general statement that admits that not everyone agrees, but reiterate that it's where you stand on the issue.

You want your audience to believe you and be on your side. Most audience members are not going to waste their time setting out to prove you wrong. They came to hear you speak for a reason. It is your responsibility not to disappoint your audience. They will give you some leeway, and the benefit of the doubt, as long as you support what you say and say it with enthusiasm and respect for your audience. But your goal is to craft your speech in such a way that there will be no need for leeway or the benefit of the doubt. As they say in sports, a handicap provides an advantage or disadvantage to someone to keep the playing field fair or to predict the winner of a contest. Your speech should not be a contest of you against them; however, your advantages are visual, vocal, and verbal preparedness. By learning to craft the perfect speech, you will not be at a disadvantage when it comes to your audience. You will be prepared and confident.

When humor fails, simply admit it and move on. If you don't, you'll look shifty and dishonest—and often, a well-placed "I guess that wasn't as funny as when I practiced in front of the mirror" will draw the laugh you were looking for. Better yet, remember: if it isn't funny, don't use it.

Finally, if you remember that nothing is 100 percent off the record, you will save yourself a lot of trouble. This goes for anyone in the public eye, but there are so many politicians in particular who need to remember this! Look at Mitt Romney. In January of 2012, the presidential hopeful made an unfortunate choice of words while advocating for consumer choice when he said, "I like being able to fire people who provide services to me." President Barack Obama isn't known for misspoken bumbling, especially on the 2012 campaign trail, but when he said, "You didn't build that," to describe how community and government working together is necessary for economic growth, he inadvertently (and let's assume unintentionally) downplayed the role of entrepreneurs and business owners. Consequently, an entire day of the Republican National Convention was themed, "You built that," and country singer Lane Turner turned the president's gaffe—or his opponent's rallying cry, depending on how you look at it—into a song. I'm sure you can remember a time when one wrong word or sentence—or in the case of Howard Dean, one wrong noise—tanked someone's career. When a reporter walks in with a television camera, remember that the audio is probably on. And when the reporter says to the cameraman, "Are you filming?" and the cameraman says, "No," the answer is probably yes. This goes for all appearances.

Whatever you say anywhere can follow you around endlessly and perhaps disastrously on YouTube and Twitter. Technology—the Internet especially—has changed the way we communicate *and* the consequences of how we communicate. The six o'clock news is full of camera-phone video footage. The media has also changed the way the audience receives the message. We're a sound-bite society; you will never get your full say. Never. Be sure you protect yourself. I think the Mayfair Madam said it best: "Never say anything on the phone you don't want your mother to hear in court." I invoke the words and wisdom of a Southern politician, the notorious Louisiana governor, Earl Long, who reputedly said: "Don't write anything you can phone. Don't phone anything you can talk. Don't talk anything you can whisper. Don't whisper anything you can smile. Don't smile anything you can nod. Don't nod anything you can wink."

Q and A

After the presentation is finished, most of the time you'll want to open the floor to questions from the audience. A moderator may help with this. The key to a successful question-and-answer component to your presentation is, firstly, to listen and, secondly, to not over answer. Keep your answers straight and to the point. Your ability as a presenter is double-checked by your skill to answer questions.

Always remember: *you* are in control. Do not give away your power. Do not let some audience member shoot you down. In a large group (or if your remarks are being recorded), always repeat the questions from the audience so everyone can hear. Be prepared to correct a questioner's mistake and restate your position. If you don't have an answer, say so and offer to get back with them if they will give you their business card. On a multiple firing line of questions—as in an angry audience member stands and asks five questions rapid-fire, back-to-back—make sure you answer one at a time as succinctly as possible. In the event it's not appropriate—or possible—for you to answer all of the inquisitor's questions, smile and say, "Whoa, that's a lot of questions. Let me take one." Never let one person run your show, but never interrupt a questioner. If the question is hostile, step toward the questioner and pull yourself up tall. There are ways to neutralize a negative audience member and prevent from stumbling.

- If you're interrupted, be politely assertive; raise your voice slightly.
- If someone put words in your mouth, correct the mistake and restate your position.
- If someone states an untruth or distorts a fact, correct the mistake and restate your position.
- If someone shoots rapid-fire questions, choose one question to answer and keep your cool.
- If an audience member demands an answer to a question that cannot be immediately answered, be politely assertive and offer to get the answer if you can.
- If someone attempts to confirm an answer while misinterpreting it or misquoting you, correct the mistake and restate your position.
- If someone asks you to respond to a controversial or critical statement, admit the bad news and bridge to your message. In some cases you ought to admit an error and quickly move on to how it has been fixed. (If it was an obvious failure of

your organization acting as if it wasn't at fault, you'll be on the front page of the paper for an extra three days.)

- If someone asks you for a personal opinion on a controversial policy, do not give personal opinions. If it's an intimate group and you can speak freely, always remember to stick with the company line.

- If someone asks your opinion of an adversary's point of view, restate your organization's position.

If you know beforehand that you'll have a hostile audience, write out the "worst case" questions you'll most likely be asked and answer them beforehand. If you've previously had a hostile question before about your topic, be sure to answer that question in your talk so you're able to negate the force when it's asked in Q and A. Ultimately, make absolutely certain that you, the presenter, have the final word.

You've put so much effort into your first, second, and third impressions that you want to make sure you walk away with a great final impression as well. Acknowledge with graciousness every member of the audience who approaches you after the speech or the Q and A. Do not look above them to find your long lost friend. Make everyone feel special. If your audience has made a connection with you during the speech, this is the perfect opportunity to maintain that connection and leave them with a positive impression.

If You're Dealing with Facts

Keep in mind that some audience members will most likely be armed with a smart phone or some other handheld device that could potentially cripple the power of your presence. How do you compete with a smart phone today? I've seen this happen; it isn't pretty. People can fact-check anything in almost less time than it takes you to say it. With the technology that a smart phone provides, an audience member can look up information and find facts in roughly seven seconds.

So, how do you prepare yourself for this type of audience member? Don't speak in generalities. If you don't know something, then just admit it, but always follow up with a genuine interest and curiosity in finding out the answer. There's no harm in prefacing your statements with "the last time I checked" or "you'd have to check the exact numbers." Your audience will not expect you to know everything, and I can guarantee that they will respond to your honesty and your desire to know more.

When a mature, adult audience is prepared to listen to a public speaker, there is a certain expectation of knowledge, within reason, that the audience and the speaker already have about the subject. Maybe you've heard stories of, or witnessed, professionals who have gotten their facts wrong in the public sphere. Ann Curry, formerly of NBC's *Today Show*, gave the commencement speech at Wheaton College in Massachusetts for which she had fact-checked information from a university in Illinois with the same name. It was quite a shock to the faculty and students when she referenced the facts of the other school, instead of their own. A stunned silence washed over students and faculty, who knew quite well that Reverend Billy Graham and Wes Craven had not gone to *their* Wheaton College. Good researchers will avoid this mishap. They will take the time to double- and triple-check the facts and will be 100 percent sure of what they are saying.

Along these lines, never put something in your speech that hasn't checked out. If you're using secondhand anecdotes, securing consent is always the right thing to do. Going back to ethos, it's absolutely imperative you fact-check anything you're planning to use in your presentation that you're offering to your audience as Truth (note the capital "T").

In his essay "The Line between Fact and Fiction," Roy Peter Clark points out, "The news media climate makes this exceedingly difficult. News cycles that used to change daily now change by the minute or even second. Cable news runs twenty-four hours a day, while more and more stories have been broken on the Internet in the middle of the night. The imperative to keep news up to the second grows stronger and stronger. Time frenzy is the enemy of clear judgment. Taking time allows for fact-checking and proportional coverage." And when it comes to using statistics and data—and you should use this in practice, not just theory—two rules apply: *Do not add* and *Do not deceive.*

Soft Landings and Transitions

Soft landings and transitions are a standard in the political world, and they are quickly taking hold of the business world. Soft landings and transitions help a speaker turn a question in the direction he or she wants to go. Remember: it's about control, and, as the speaker, *you're* in control. You can take any soft landing and pair it with any transition if you remember the golden rule: *never* say "but" or "however" (the only time you can say "but" is if what you're saying is reminiscent of letting your audience in on a secret). It's easier than it sounds. Simply choose a phrase on the left from the soft landings column and go directly to the transitions column on the right.

Soft Landings	*Transitions*
• I agree with you.	• First, let me say . . .
• You make an interesting point.	• I don't have that information, but I can tell you . . .
• I appreciate your position.	• You should also know that . . .
• I understand your point of view.	• Let me explain . . .
• I can see where you are coming from.	• I'm also frequently asked . . . • Let me add . . .
• Many people I have spoken to feel as you do.	• A common concern is . . .
• Yes, we need to look into that more carefully.	• For example . . . • Equally importantly . . .
• Your point is well taken.	• One point I believe the audience would be interested in . . .
• I can see why you would think that way.	• You can go one step further . . .

I like to use these because I'm Southern. These phrases are very polite-sounding but I still get to go where I was going anyway, maintaining my power and choice of direction. That's the whole point of soft landings and transitions; they help you change the direction of the conversation to put you back in a position of power. If you spend an hour watching Sunday morning political talk shows, you'll receive a quick tutorial in soft landings and transitions. I'm not sure where this list originated but it is a standard training we use for elected officials.

Sometimes you will have to redirect a conversation back to about the topic of your presentation, or you may need to familiarize your audience with your subject matter. Here are some good phrases that not only help set the tone but also help keep your listeners engaged:

- I'm not sure what your dad said, but mine always told me
- Consider this
- You know what it's like
- Remember the time
- In fact
- Interestingly enough
- It's important to understand

These not only help set the tone but also help continue to engage your listeners.

Staying Current

After every public event, reexamine your presentations, speeches, and topics to make sure they meet that particular audience's needs and expectations. Remember that things change and you don't want to be outside the loop. The presentation you gave last year at orientation may need to be tweaked to reach the new members in your group. Words and well-known sayings you've used in the past do come and go, so make sure that your antidotes, stories, and jargon are in line with current topics and trends.

In order to do this, you must read and keep up on new trends. Be careful that you don't rely year after year, speech after speech, on the same old topics and stories and facts and figures. Watch the news and read the newspaper. You need to be the most intelligent person you can be. Read and research and study and surf the web to see what others are saying now. It's important because your audience is fed a twenty-four hour news cycle, seven days a week, and many of them think they are smarter than you, which may or may not be true.

As a professional public speaker, I had to give similar presentations for several years in the political circuit. Today, I don't give those speeches because the campaigns are run differently now. I built a great career on these speeches and topics. I made myself known by giving the same type of presentation several times over, but in today's social media saturation, these old speeches would come across as irrelevant, or worse, uninformed. So much has changed, and as a result, I had to rethink my theme, my content, and my message. You can use the same basic speechwriting principles from this book every time you need to update your content. If you haven't looked over your presentation in a while, definitely do so before you speak, especially if you want to be known as someone in the know.

This can apply to changes in your own life as well. One overweight speaker I know had a truckload of funny fat jokes. He used his obesity as a way to make the audience laugh, and it worked for him. He was a big boy, so he could get away with it. When he ran into some health issues, he lost a ton of weight, which is a wonderful thing. However, he can no longer use the same old fat jokes. They are not funny anymore because he's not fat and someone could misinterpret what he is saying; rather than poking fun at himself, he could innocently pick an audience member as the victim of his jokes. So, my colleague is finding new material now that he is thin. His health depends on it, and so does his career. Make sure you do the same; as your situation and your environment changes, adjust your material to reflect your new surroundings.

Remember, although they are your audience, it's *your* responsibility to adapt to them. They came to see *you*, listen to *your* speech, and be moved by *your* words. So whether you're adapting to a falling ceiling, managing a Q and A from a hostile audience, or using a transition to guide the conversation to where you want it to go, because you've prepared and fine-tuned your voice, your look, and your content, you will be able to maintain control and deliver the rock star performance they came to see.

8

THIS IS ROCK STAR

Those who tell stories rule the world.

—PLATO

If your favorite musician simply came out on stage and performed your favorite song without dancing around a bit, moving about the stage, or using facial expressions or body movements to interpret the song for you and to entertain the audience, then you might say to yourself, "Why did I pay seventy-five dollars to come hear this musician perform this song? I could have listened to it in the privacy of my own home." People pay a lot of money to go to concerts and to see their favorite musicians perform on stage, not because they don't have the music at home but because they want to see a *performance*. It is then the rock star's responsibility to provide that experience to avoid disappointing his or her audience. How can the rock star guarantee a satisfied audience? He can *perform* the audience's favorite songs, rather than just playing them, and can respond to the vibes from the audience. Think of you and your speech in the same way—the rock star and the rock concert. You are the performer. Now, perform for your audience.

This is the hardest part for most of us. You may need to bring additional enthusiasm to your speech to wake up an otherwise sleepy, uninvolved audience. Remember, though, sometimes you'll need to fake it until you become it. There will be times when you need to put on that bigger-than-big smile just to wow your audience. Remember, your goal is always to engage your audience with what you say. *How* you say it goes a long way toward doing that.

Don't misunderstand me when I say you've got to fake it until you become it. Remember, you should never fake information, your own level of knowledge, your background, or your experiences. Just keep in mind that it's okay to perform your enthusiasm, your confidence, and your interest in a particular topic. Don't feel that you are being dishonest in doing so; just take that performance to convince yourself of your own enthusiasm, confidence, and interest. Paulo Coelho puts it like this: "You must be the person you have never had the courage to be. Gradually, you will discover that you are that person, but until you can see this clearly, you must pretend and invent."

One of the best ways to learn how to perform your speech is to watch others do it. In the following pages, I've highlighted several contemporary speeches I came across in my own research. These fine examples reiterate many of the salient topics I've previously discussed and demonstrate the qualities to which I have referred throughout this book. I found many of these great speeches on a website called TED: Ideas Worth Spreading. This proved to be a fantastic tool for me to review whole speeches on a wide range of subjects. If you can't find one of the speeches I have cited on TED, then search for them on YouTube or Vimeo, two more great resources for watching rock star performances of audio and visual digital recordings.

Spoilers

Providing your audience with an agenda—also known as a spoiler alert—of what'll be happening during your presentation is smart. This doesn't have to be in writing, just spoken. It's a part of the "tell them what you're going to tell them, tell them what you told them" approach. If you don't have a hugely over-the-top transformative claim to impart to your audience, providing them with this sort of verbal roadmap makes a difference. Start by telling them the objective of your speech. What is it that you hope they will gain? Then, at the end of your speech, you can reiterate that objective and test the audiences', or your own, understanding of how you reached your objective.

Steve Jobs' 2005 commencement address at Stanford University is a great example of telling the audience what's about to happen. It begins like this: "Today I want to tell you three stories from my life. That's it. No big deal. Just three stories." In those brief sentences, he describes exactly what he has in store for his audience. He's not overly flowery, and he gets to the point. You'll likely find that audiences have a tendency to respond to this sort of direction.

Randy Pausch's "Last Lecture" is another example of providing the audience with a roadmap of what's about to happen: "Today's talk is about my childhood dreams and how I achieved them. How I believe I've been able to enable the dream of others, and lessons learned." Though it's in a similar vein, Pausch offers a slightly grander mission. Audiences will also often respond to this sort of prompting.

Since your audience's attention span is short, even on the best of days, do yourself a favor by letting them know what is coming for presentations that are longer than one hour. Remember that audiences like to be assured that during your time together you will focus on three main points and end early enough for them to be first in line at the cocktail hour, to arrive at Macy's before it closes, or catch the early train home. This will let the audience know that you respect their busy schedules.

Anything for a Laugh

Knowing how to use humor correctly can give your speech new life, and make audiences sit up and pay attention. Much of the success or failure of humor is due to timing. Ellen DeGeneres' 2009 commencement speech to the graduating "Katrina class" at New Orleans' Tulane University is a fine example of this:

> *As you grow, you'll realize the definition of success changes. For many of you, today, success is being able to hold down twenty shots of tequila. For me, the most important thing in your life is to live your life with integrity, and not to give into peer pressure. To try to be something that you're not. To live your life as an honest and compassionate person, to contribute in some way. So to conclude my conclusion: follow your passion, stay true to yourself. Never follow anyone else's path, unless you're in the woods and you're lost and you see a path, and by all means you should follow that.*

Of course, we all expect Ellen DeGeneres to be funny. And, again, it's definitely a great speech to review for guidance on comedic timing; so is "Ken Robinson Says Schools Kill Creativity." In his profoundly moving case for creating an education system that nurtures creativity, his wit is front and center. I take that back—it's more than wit. I laughed out loud, which is curious since his presentation covers some serious stuff. That's often the point. A truly gifted orator can use humor to help the audience navigate even the most alarming information.

Leave Nothing to Chance

Do you remember when I told you never to forget when you are in control? That's true not only when you're delivering your speech but also when you're writing it. In Majora Carter's "Greening the Ghetto" speech for TED, she tells the audience exactly what they need to know. There's no mistaking her take-home message; there's no room for interpretation. She tells her audience exactly what they're supposed to derive from her presentation. She also says more in eighteen minutes and thirty-three seconds then most people say all week.

Next, take a look at the provocative six-minute TED talk "A Sense of Humor about Afghanistan? Artist Aman Mojadidi Shows How." Aman Mojadidi calls himself "Afghan by blood, redneck by the grace of god." He boldly conveys these two dichotic identities through his art—and in his presentation. He's unerring in what he wants his listeners to walk away with. Until the end, he holds his audience in what could be described as rapt calm; he knows exactly where he plans to take the audience, so even while there's a bit of a twist at the end, his listeners know what they're in for along the way.

Being confident, bold, and unapologetic about whatever your speech is about is essential in order to get an audience to wake up and listen—and to believe what you're saying. It leaves no room for doubt. It also inspires the audience to have confidence in you—that you know what you're talking about, and that you know your craft as a speaker. Compelling, riveting speeches are all cut from this same cloth.

Do the Extraordinary

Being unforgettable often means keeping audiences on their toes. It also helps you avoid ever coming across as stale, boring, or worn-out. Jodie Foster's 2006 commencement speech at University of Pennsylvania is a great example of doing the unexpected. Near the end of her speech, she makes this poignant offering:

> *All of that fine and delicious matter has a way of becoming the material of your life. You pick up bits and pieces of treasure and trash, pain and pleasure, passions and disappointments, and you start stuffing them in your bag . . . your big bag of experience. You do some dumb things that don't work out at all. You stumble excitedly on little gems that you never saw coming. And you stuff them all in your bag. You pursue the things you love and believe in. You cast off the images of yourself that don't fit. And suddenly you look behind you and a pattern emerges. You look in front of you and the path makes sense. There is nothing more beautiful than finding your course as you believe you bob aimlessly in the current. Wouldn't you know that your path was there all along, waiting for you to knock, waiting for you to become. This path does not belong to your parents, your teachers, your leaders, or your lovers. Your path is your character defining itself more and more every day like a photograph coming into focus, like a color that becomes more vivid in contrast with its surroundings.*

After this remarkable human effort, the Oscar-winning actress ends her address with the chorus of Eminem's "Lose Yourself" from *8 Mile*, the semiautobiographical film released in 2002. No one saw it coming. And, yes, the audience was captivated. As a lesson to you: whether it's taking the time to find a special quote from someone your audience might not anticipate or having a strange surprise something-something, consider taking a chances with the rock star entertainment factor of your presentation.

Effective Use of Props

I've said it before and I'll keep saying it: forget overloading your audience with facts and figures and smart data; keep it simple, use anecdotes, have a clear message that features a beginning, middle, and end—it's that simple. For years people insisted that speakers use technology to enhance their presentations. It's my opinion that an audience would much rather be subject to a candid personality than a computer screen, but if you need a digital image, then use it effectively.

Jill Bolte Taylor does a good job of optimizing PowerPoint in her TED talk "Stroke of Insight." Yes, it's true. She uses PowerPoint (to a minimum). Even better, her presentation is a stellar example of using visual aides. She actually brings a *human brain* to the stage. It's a shocking, utterly unforgettable showstopper. Perhaps even more rewarding for the audience is her use of gestures and body language, as well as her ability to tell her own story. She does all of this sans notes.

Simon Sinek, former anthropology student and author of *Start with Why*, forgoes PowerPoint in his speech "How Great Leaders Inspire Action" but shows us that writing on large pieces of paper can be powerful stuff. Not only does it help elicit and secure audience involvement, it keeps the energy moving. He codified what he calls "the golden circle" to describe his theory that people don't buy *what* you do; they buy *why* you do it. As he draws simple images—literally circles, lines, and a few numbers—on sheets of an Office Depot white flip-pad, he continues to describe his research on the brain and offer insight on the "why" of success.

Next, take a look at Caitria and Morgan O'Neill's "How to Step Up in the Face of Disaster." They begin their presentation with news footage of a freak tornado that hit their Massachusetts hometown. They then offer photos taken of the aftermath that convey the gravity of the situation. They tell the audience, "Armed with two laptops and an aircard, we built a recovery machine." Following this they have a title image that states, "The O'Neill Sisters Present: Monson Tornado in 60 Seconds." At which point they perform a narrative skit. All of it works, all of it resonates, and all of it—especially the three graphs they use—helps them teach their audience about a new initiative in disaster recovery.

Being Frank

People love it when you're honest with them. I don't mean what you really think about their outfit or hair color or choice of spouse. I mean when you speak honestly to something that resonates with them— when you have found a truth that is so wonderful it's worth sharing because it turns convention on its head and does away with cliché. That kind of truth is something people can work with, something that makes them nod their heads and say, "Yes, that's exactly how I feel! That's my experience, too! I thought I was the only one."

Ray Bradbury does a great job of showing how to capture candor (and exuberance) in "Sixth Annual Writer's Symposium by the Sea."

I want your loves to be multiple. I don't want you to be a snob about anything. Anything you love, you do it. It's got to be with a great sense of fun. Writing is not a serious business. It's a joy and a celebration. You should be having fun with it. Ignore the authors who say, "Oh, my God, what word?" you know. Now, to hell with that. It's not work. If it's work, stop and do something else.

Now, what I'm thinking of is people always saying, "Well, what do we do about a sudden blockage in your writing? What if you have a blockage and you don't know what to do about it?" Well, it's obvious you're doing the wrong thing, isn't it? In the middle of writing something you go blank and your mind says: "No, that's it." Ok. You're being warned, aren't you? Your subconscious is saying, "I don't like you anymore. You're writing about things I don't give a damn for." You're being political, or you're being socially aware. You're writing things that will benefit the world. To hell with that! I don't write things to benefit the world. If it happens that they do, swell. I didn't set out to do that. I set out to have a hell of a lot of fun.

I've never worked a day in my life. I've never worked a day in my life. The joy of writing has propelled me from day to day and year to year. I want you to envy me, my joy. Get out of here tonight and say: "Am I being joyful?" And if you've got a writer's block, you can cure it this evening by stopping whatever you're writing and doing something else. You picked the wrong subject.

Even though we've tried to cover it up in many ways, I believe it's a natural human instinct to tell the truth, and I think it's a natural human instinct that people respond to it. And I realize that people speak for all sorts of different reasons—your presentation might be about conveying to your top managers why layoffs are necessary. In that vein, it's impossible for me to say you will *always* need to believe in what you say. The point I'd like to make is that there's no doubt in my mind most audiences have built-in lie detectors. They'll be able to sense your commitment to what you say; so, if it's possible, be vested in your message.

Even if it's something akin to "I don't like this any more than you do," speak your mind and share your sincerity with your listeners. The power of the response you receive may surprise you.

Take Your Time

Whether you choke up when discussing something emotional or stumble with sentiment or passion, never be or feel rushed. There are times when a dramatic pause shows your sincerity for the topic at hand. Candy Chang does this in "Before I die I want to..." as she speaks of a mentor whose death spurred her to dive into community art projects and lead a better, more productive life. Her hesitation is charming. It's not uncomfortable for the audience, and it helps endear her to them.

Joel Burns, during a televised city council meeting in Fort Worth, Texas, in October 2010, shares his emotion in his twelve-minute speech in which he tells gay teens "it gets better." Here, too, a "pause of emotion" shows the audience that a rash of teen suicides affects him. He moves through this emotion—he moves beyond it—to continue his presentation, but that unintended pause of emotion shows his sincerity.

In a similar vein, giving a eulogy can be especially tough. Not feeling rushed is the best advice. Controlled emotion is key; if you feel tears well up, count backwards from five and take a deep breath. Remember, too, that your audience—especially at a funeral—will, most likely, be empathetic to what you're going through.

Audience Involvement

Including your listeners in your presentation in an active way can be especially rewarding for them—and you. Jane McGonigal does a rock star job of involving her audience in "Gaming Can Make a

Better World." She challenges the audience with a mission: the mission is to increase every single audience member's lifespan by seven and a half minutes. She's droll about it—what they should do with their seven-and-a-half minutes and why she's on this mission. Her brand of humor works, and by including the audience in the mission, she paves the way for their undivided attention.

As one might expect, so does Bobby McFerrin. He's a natural performer, but he's completely on his game when he "plays" his audience at the World Science Fair in 2010. He creates an imagery makeshift piano along the edge of the stage that prompts his audience to carry a lively tune. As he jumps and leaps from left to right along and back, he harmonizes to his audience's singing for a memorable three-minute performance.

Another bit of prowess is to use improvisation. Go ahead and have fun, be spontaneous—enjoy the moment-to-moment experience of public speaking and presentation giving. As you grow more and more comfortable as a speaker, you'll often find that you're more likely to use improvisation and talk back and forth with your audience. Usman Riaz and Preston Reed do this in "A Young Guitarist Meets His Hero" when the two musicians take on a spur-of-the-moment bit of improv. Beth Moore, founder of Living Proof Ministries, excels at this in her conferences and videos for women. She talks with her audience, so while she controls the stage and the microphone, there's a genuine sense that none of the journey she takes with her audience is necessarily planned—even when they are prerecorded.

Three Lessons to Support Theory

In novelist Chimamanda Adichie's TED presentation "The Danger of a Single Story," she does a number of things right. She uses humor, she offers a personal story to prove her point, and she has three lessons to support her theory. It's this latter point that makes her essential research for our purposes. Notice the way she articulates her lessons. As a storyteller, she's adept at timing and action. I'm sure she left a few details out—and that's important. When you're crafting your stories, make certain they move along fluidly and quickly. Providing too many details slows down the action—and remember: the overuse of adverbs is a sign of a weak vocabulary.

Mentioned above for his whiteboard ways, Simon Sinek also provides a fine example of the magic of three. In "How Great Leaders Inspire Action," he uses Apple, Martin Luther King, and the Wright brothers to make his point. Steve Jobs does it, too—and, look, that's three.

Rather than "I, I, I"

Let others who've affected or enriched your life help you to tell the story. Rather than saying "I, I, I," find stories from others that help you share your message. This is especially effective with younger audiences. Randy Pausch's "Last Lecture" also offers a fine example of using such anecdotal narratives to convey what someone else was able to point out. As a lesson from his mentor Andy Van Dam (Randy was Van Dam's teaching assistant at Brown University), Randy states, "Andy put his arm around my shoulders and we went for a little walk and he said, 'Randy, it's such a shame that people perceive you as so arrogant, because it's going to limit what you're going to be able to accomplish in life.'" Having enlisted Andy in making his point, Randy sealed the deal that his audience would find him humble and gracious. When crafting your speech, look for opportunities to let others help you teach.

Looking again to "Ken Robinson Says Schools Kill Creativity," we see an example of this. With his main premise that "If you're not prepared to be wrong, you'll never come up with anything original," his presentation offers us a great example of how to use a third-person story effectively. In this case, he shares the story of Gillian Lynne. Lynne is a choreographer who's best known for the musicals *Cats* and *The Phantom of the Opera*. He tells his audience how she became a dancer. In his retelling of her story, he does everything right. He provides just enough detail to move the anecdote along quickly and efficiently. He also uses language that's imagistic; he uses words that evoke animation. There's little doubt that Robinson chose the very best, most exacting story to promote his premise. In this case, he didn't need three stories; he needed one—Lynne's.

When you sit down to begin crafting your presentation, I want to you to keep these examples in mind. What stood out to you? Which one of these speakers' style most resembled yours? Don't be afraid to learn from those who have gone before you. Stand on the shoulders of those giants, but don't forget who you are and what makes you special. Originality is what happens when you forget what it means to be afraid.

9

CONFESSIONS OF A ROCK STAR SPEAKER

As an executive speech and corporate presentations coach, I've been on the road for twenty years, and I still love what I do because the results are undeniable. I can often see within a short period of time that my audience, or my students, will be better off because of what I have shared with them on any particular day. I feel confident about what I do, and it is rewarding to know that I have helped someone to craft a new beginning, a new approach, or eased them gently toward to another opportunity. I know that public speaking is hard for some people, but I hold fast to the claim that if you apply the tips and suggestions that I have discussed in this book, it will become easier, and with time you, too, can be a rock star public speaker.

I believe that if you wish to begin, develop, or maintain a career as a speaker, you must love what you do. You must also love your topic, your company, and your audience (or at least pretend that you do). Enjoy the courage this takes, and trust that you are changing others with your words. You are making an impact on their perspectives, thoughts, and opinions. That is what speakers do. Whether your impact is strong, weak, or ambiguous is up to you. However, when you focus on what it takes to be an expert in your field, you will naturally grow in wisdom and knowledge, and when you have mastery of a topic you love, you can share your knowledge more easily. *Don't pull the ladder up, but help others up the ladder.* In other words, don't take your knowledge with you; impart it to those who are willing to listen. Your voice matters, and it will inspire others to great successes of their own.

I know that with practice, time, and proficiency, the skills you have gleaned in reading this book will help you succeed. You may be wondering how you can take the information you have learned and put it into practice, how you can acquire speaking engagements. Develop a specialty, and then find a network to promote your ideas and yourself. If you are an accountant, doctor, lawyer, cook, teacher, writer, or musician, find industry-specific magazines or publications and market yourself. Start by writing and sending an article, a commentary, or a letter to the editor. Practice your message and don't stop until you've gotten it published on a website, in a journal, or in a magazine. It could turn into a column, or you may decide you want to write a blog. If you're not confident in your writing, have someone edit your work. It's always beneficial to have a second pair of eyes take a look.

Your online presence and publications will give you creditability and enrich your reputation if you are trying to move into a professional role as a public speaker. By doing this, when you go to pitch a topic for a conference to be a speaker or a breakout presenter, you can send copies of your work or mention it in your bio that you are a contributor to XYZ magazine, which will help solidify your standing as a known expert in your chosen field.

Writing an op-ed every once in a while is another great idea to show your passion and zeal for a particular topic. However, try not to do so on a regular basis. This might communicate that you have the time to argue with something you saw in the newspaper because you don't have enough paying gigs. This is the mark of an amateur. Find your audience, stick within your network, and your speaking will grow organically and sustainably.

I am a huge fan of local conferences like TEDx, Pecha-Kucha, or other tech or literary stage performances. Groups such as these now have local chapters in many cities, and it is possible to get chosen as a presenter if you follow the right protocol. This will give you a good entry to the public forum, especially if you are a beginner, and allow you to debut to a home crowd. Research what is available in your area. If there is nothing, find something close by and try to emulate it in your city or town. Don't wait on others to build your stage.

Within your established network of professionals, you may offer to serve on a panel that needs an expert. You may also offer to emcee the panel or to emcee other events within your community. Offer to lead in your civic clubs and social circles. It's up to you how much you're willing to give away before you can make your mark to speak, but if you need the practice and the exposure, don't avoid opportunities to speak just because you aren't getting paid. They will not only give you practice, they will likely provide feedback, and if you follow through with the principles outlined in this book and people like what you have to say, your reputation will grow naturally.

Remember to network with your audience, too. You never know when you might meet someone who would like for you to speak at another event. I cannot count how many gigs I have gotten because I networked before and after a conference in which I was the presenter. However, do not seek out the next job when the current job is paying you. That would be unfair to your hiring agent. You may choose to mention that you're available or offer a way to get in touch, but no more: there can be no blatant advertising. Your audience will understand that you can come to their next conference, but be careful that you don't harm your relationship with those who brought you in this time. Those who have already paid you for your time deserve your loyalty much more than someone in your audience who may or may not have the say to hire you for another conference. Keep in touch with the people and organizations that hired you. You never know if they will need you again.

Once on the ground at a conference, if they are kind to me and easy to work with, I may offer to do another event at the conference. As a speaker, sometimes you're chattel, so do what you can to accommodate the invitee's needs. This might mean acting as a moderator for a discussion or introducing another speaker. If I'm already there, I know the audience and the organization, and I love what I do so it is easy for me to give a little extra. You will hear many different opinions about this practice, but do what you think is best. Don't give yourself, your talent, or your hard work away for nothing, or there will be no need to hire you again. One mark of a great speaker is to be hired again by the same group.

Depending on where you are, who you are, and who knows you, your fees may vary. Be careful that you're consistent when accepting a fair price because no matter what people say (Oh, I'll keep your "special" price just between us), I guarantee word will get out.

Recently, I found myself in this sticky wicket. I live in a small state so it's not hard to find out who pays what. A friend came to town to speak and asked me to fill out the agenda. Because the group only had so much money for us, this friend offered to fill in the rest of my fee. On paper, however, it looked like I was paid less than my standard fee, so I got caught in a tough place with good folks who had hard feelings because they wanted my lower fee (which didn't exist) instead of my standard fee.

No matter how hard it is, pass on opportunities that offer you less than you feel you deserve, or less than you can afford. Some organizations may offer you a smaller fee but include other incentives. For example, you can consider lowering your fee if the group you would like to speak for will let you run an ad for a year in their magazine or on their website. The hiring company may also list you as a logoed sponsor for their other events, or they may ask you to write a column for their publication with a bi-line that says you're available to speak to groups. Think about how you can structure financial opportunities in future speaking jobs rather than in cash. Bartering is a great way to gain access to perks that were once unavailable to you.

Speaking is a challenging business, and getting paid for it can be difficult for many reasons. However, I believe that the reward is worth the effort, and what you'll learn in the process will give you a lifetime of memories, and in many cases true friends. Remember, no one brings to the table what you bring to the table. Your gift is what you have to share, and you never know how your words will change the world. I titled this book *Speak Without Fear*, not because you'll never have fear, but now you know the secret to controlling your fear in order to let the best you shine through. Beneath that layer of fear that has been collecting for years is an original voice with a powerful message. Don't allow doubt to cloud your performance. Doubt is the manifestation of others' insecurities that have been placed on you. Shrug off those preconceived notions of unworthiness; you deserve to be heard, and if you are prepared, confident, and energetic, there will be no denying the fact that *you* are a rock star.

ACKNOWLEDGEMENTS

You should write a book... they all said.

I've heard that a thousand times and every time I'd reply that there were plenty of public speaking books on the market and the world didn't need another one!

There is not one like yours.

I told them thank you but No... I didn't have the time. And then one friend said something I'll never forget, *Deb, what I don't want... is to sit here a year from now and you still not have your book.* So about a year later with those words still ringing in my ear I called my friend back and committed to doing the work to write a book.

They say it takes a village...in my case it took a small nation to get me where I needed to go. And I have the most amazing tribe that helped me make it happen. Not only my publishing team but also my friends who have encouraged me to get this done. To be so lucky to have friends who care that I complete what I start - thank you.

A special shout out for my friends with beach houses that invited me to stop and rest and write—the Stevens, the Clyborne's and the Benedicts—you have no idea what the salt water and air does for my soul—thank you.

My thanks would not be complete without an acknowledgment to the campaign schools and conferences where I teach who remind me that if we're going to leave our mark in this world we have no options but to learn to Speak Without Fear if we're going to change our city, state, nation, country or simply ourselves.

I am forever honored to have led the Women's Campaign School at Yale for three years as President of the Board and as the public speaking trainer for the past 12 years. The friends I have made from my time at Yale I cannot begin to count, from the amazing students who changed me into being a better leader to the board who believed and supported our mission and me to renewed success. I'd like to thank Patti Russo my dear Italian sister your friendship, support, love and kindness knows no bounds and I am forever grateful our paths crossed. Nancy Bocskor, the reason I was considered for Yale in the first place thank you for your belief in me and for our friendship through the years. Pam Stark, our third musketeer, for keeping it all in check with great humor and love as we redirected the ship to sail.

And to the amazing women who I speak to year after year at the John F. Kennedy School of Government at Harvard University—*from*

Harvard Square to the Oval Office Program under the visionary leadership of Victoria Budson. The opportunity to be a part of the wonderful program is a dream come true and the connection to women who will change the world is exciting to partner with as they go forth and Speak Without Fear.

I am blessed to speak around the world for International Republican Institute and the Women's Democracy Network. The opportunities to help women in other countries find their voice and learn to use it—is why I leave my home, pack my bags, sit in airports, train stations and bus stops to explain the concept of Speaking Without Fear when your voice is the only one speaking up for those who have no voice. With appreciation to Judy Van Rest the amazing staff at IRI.

There are so many other amazing friends and colleagues who have helped in my journey to have the stories and insights into what it takes to Speak Without Fear I could not begin to list all the names in a book but please know that I am forever grateful.

I readily admit that none of this would be possible without the quiet strength of my family. To my brother Sam and his partner Brian for expecting great things from the little sister and my brothers David and Joel who will be surprised.

And especially my Mom and Dad who gave me wings to fly and then let me go.

And thank you for choosing this book to begin your journey to believe that you can learn to Speak Without Fear. You are on your way.

This book is dedicated to my Mom and Dad

Mary and Sam Vause

who believe in me

and always have.

There is no greater gift a parent can instill than the confidence to believe that everything is possible—thank you.

ABOUT THE AUTHOR

Deb Sofield is an award-winning speaker, radio talk show host, presenter, and executive speech coach who trains men and women around the world for success in public speaking, presentation skills, and message development. A former press secretary and advertising executive, she understands what audiences and interviewers expect from presenters and public figures. As a coach, Deb prepares her clients for presentations, interviews, and road shows and has advised members of congress, secretaries of state, and numerous other elected officials and industry leaders. Working as a publicist, Sofield has managed print, television, and radio media relations, directed corporate and campaign publicity, and implemented crisis management plans.

Deb's passion is helping professionals succeed in the modern business arena. As a speaker, she addresses audiences nationwide on Public Speaking Skills for the Professional™, an intensive public speaking and presentation class especially for corporate clients and The Unspoken Rules of the Game™, a lively discussion on the bad habits that hold women back in business and life. Her other acclaimed speeches include 15 Rules for the Road—A Public Speaking Primer™, The Art of the Interview™ and Media Savvy Presentations™. Her work as a speaker, trainer and coach has earned Deb recognition as Communicator of the Year by the Association for Women in Communications. From a lifetime of experience in politics, business and travel, Sofield instructions, enables and inspires audiences to achieve their very best.

Known for her lively speaking style, Sofield is also esteemed for the impact of her work. Deb Sofield is a visiting professor, teaching public speaking at Harvard University, John F. Kennedy School of Government. She is a past president of the board and current speaker for the Woman's Campaign School at Yale University. She is a featured presenter for the University of South Carolina's School of Journalism and Mass Communications, Clemson University's Self Civic Fellows program at the Strom Thurmond Institute of Government and Public Affairs and the Ethics in Government program, also at Clemson. Sofield also works with the International Republican Institute of Washington, DC and served as a mentor and trainer for the Center for Liberty in the Middle East (CLIME).

Beyond just business and politics, Deb is a recognized public servant and respected community leader. The Governor of South Carolina paid tribute to her with the award of the Order of the Palmetto, South Carolina's highest honor. Additionally, Sofield was chosen as one of Greenville, South Carolina's Best & Brightest, was selected by GSA Business Journal as one of the area's Most Influential Women in Business and was awarded the Order of the Jessamine for her outstanding leadership and service to the community. She is recognized for both her work in improving the lives of others and her contributions to the state of South Carolina, the southern region, the nation and the world and was honored by Leadership South Carolina with the Legacy of Leadership Award. Deb is considered one of South Carolina's most formidable women; the Southeastern Institute for Women in Politics awarded Deb Sofield the Leading Women Award. She won the prestigious Toastmasters District 58 Communication and Leadership Award, the Strom Thurmond Excellence in Public Service honor and was chosen as the ATHENA Award recipient by the Chamber of Commerce. Recently, Deb was selected as a YWCA Woman of Achievement.

Deb holds a bachelor of arts in public speaking. She is a graduate of Leadership America, the Women's Campaign School at Yale University and a Liberty Fellow—a South Carolina partnership with the Aspen Institute. Sofield is also a member of the National Speakers Association.

RECOMMENDED READING

Selling the Dream by Guy Kawaski, Harper Business.

Simply Speaking by Peggy Noonan, Harper Collins.

14,000 Quips and Quotes for Writers and Speakers by E. C. McKenzie, Greenwich House.

See You at the Top by Zig Ziglar, Pelican.

Podium Humor by James C. Humes, Harper & Row.

Speakers Sourcebook by Eleanor Doan, Zondervan.

The 21 Irrefutable Laws of Leadership by John Maxwell, Nelson.

Why You Say It by Webb Garrison, MJF Books.

Speakers Library of Business by Joe Griffith, Prentice Hall.

The New York Public Library Book of 20th Century American Quotations, Warner Books.

Secrets of a CEO Coach by Debra Benton, McGraw Hill.

Your Public Best by Lillian Brown, New Market Press.